The Power of Simplicity

The Power of Simplicity

A MANAGEMENT GUIDE TO CUTTING THROUGH THE NONSENSE AND DOING THINGS RIGHT

JACK TROUT

with **STEVE RIVKIN**

McGraw-Hill

NEW YORK   SAN FRANCISCO   WASHINGTON, D.C.   AUCKLAND   BOGOTÁ
CARACAS   LISBON   LONDON   MADRID   MEXICO CITY   MILAN
MONTREAL   NEW DELHI   SAN JUAN   SINGAPORE
SYDNEY   TOKYO   TORONTO

Library of Congress Cataloging-in-Publication Data

Trout, Jack.
 The power of simplicity : a management guide to cutting through the nonsense and
doing things right/Jack Trout with Steve Rivkin.
  p. cm.
 Includes bobliographical reference and index.
 ISBN 0-07-065362-3
 1. Industrial management. 2. Simplicity. I. Rivkin, Steve. II. Title.
HD31. T689 1999
 658.8—dc21   98-37927
                         CIP

1 2 3 4 5 6 7 8 9 0 DOC/DOC 9 0 3 2 1 0 9 8

ISBN 0-07-065362-3

*The sponsoring editor for this book was Mary Glenn, the editing supervisor was Penny Linskey,
the designer was Michael Mendelsohn of M M Design 2000, Inc., and the production supervisor was
Pamela A. Pelton. It was set in ITC Bookman by M M Design 2000, Inc.*

Printed and bound by R. R. Donnelley & Sons Company.

McGraw-Hill books are available at special quantity discounts to use as premiums and sales promotions, or for use in corporate training programs. For more information, please write to the
Director of Special Sales, McGraw-Hill, 11 West 19th Street, New York, NY 10011. Or contact
your local bookstore.

This book is printed on acid-free paper.

DEDICATED TO THE
OVERWHELMED AND THE CONFUSED
WHO SENSE THERE'S A
SIMPLER WAY

Contents

PEOPLE ISSUES

IN CONCLUSION

Introduction

Some years ago, while John Sculley was still head of Apple Computer, he gave a speech that contained what we consider a brilliant observation: *"Everything we have learned in the industrial age has tended to create more and more complication. I think that more and more people are learning that you have to simplify, not complicate. Simplicity is the ultimate sophistication."*

Unfortunately for John, he didn't pay quite enough attention to what he said and he bet his reputation on an overcomplicated product called the Newton which was dubbed a "personal digital assistant." None of this was very simple. The product failed and John was fired.

But Mr. Sculley was on to something. On-rushing technology, rapid communications, the complex global economy, and the ever-increasing pace of business have created an environment that is clouding people's minds.

It's no wonder that many companies are turning to one consulting organization after another looking for help or clarity, or that so many executives are going back to school or seeking out the self-help crowd for enlightenment on how to be a success. And there is no shortage of people willing to take their money.

Well, ladies and gentlemen, business is not that complex. It's just that there are too many people out there making it complex. The way to fight complexity is to use simplicity. As Mr. Sculley intimated, the future belongs to the simpleminded.

In an attempt to gain perspective on this problem, we went backward to what we thought were simpler times. But we soon learned that noted thinkers have been preaching about the importance of simplicity for decades. (You'll see many of them quoted throughout the book.) In other words, the problem of complexity appears to have always been with us. It's part of the human condition.

It struck us that it was time to take another run at that windmill of complexity that business continues to get swept up in. And to take a simple look at the basic business practices that are endlessly discussed, written about, consulted on, agonized over, and, sometimes, just plain screwed up.

This effort takes in big issues such as leadership and organization as well as the everyday problems of pricing and marketing. In each case we try to get to the essence of how to get it right.

We guarantee you that somewhere in this book you'll find insights into how your life can get a lot simpler and your business more effective.

JACK TROUT

The Power of Simplicity

The Basics of Simplicity

....

Some people fear it, but you can begin to think and talk in simple terms.

CHAPTER 1

Simplicity

Why people fear it so much

Simple Simon met a pieman going to the fair.
Said Simple Simon to the pieman,
Let me see your ware.
Says the pieman to Simple Simon,
Show me first your penny.
Says Simple Simon to the pieman,
Indeed, I have not any.

— Mother Goose

Through the years, being called "simple" was never a plus. And being called "simpleminded" or a "simpleton" was downright negative. It meant you were stupid, gullible, or feebleminded. It's no wonder that people fear being simple.

We call it the curse of "Simple Simon."

When psychologists are asked about this fear, they get a little more complex. (Not surprising.) Psychologist John Collard of the Institute of Human Relations at Yale University described seven kinds of common fears. (All of us have some of them.)

1. Fear of failure
2. Fear of sex
3. Fear of self-defense
4. Fear of trusting others
5. Fear of thinking
6. Fear of speaking
7. Fear of being alone

It would appear that not being simple—or not seeking simple solutions—stems from number 5, "fear of thinking."

The problem is that instead of thinking things through for ourselves, we rely on the thinking of others. (This is why the worldwide management consulting business is expected to grow to about $114 billion by the year 2000.)

Says Dr. Collard: "Not only is it hard work to think, but many people fear the activity itself. They are docile and obedient and easily follow suggestions put forward by others, because it saves them the labor of thinking for themselves. They become dependent on others for headwork, and fly to a protector when in difficulty."

This fear of thinking is having a profound impact in the business of news. Some even wonder whether it has much of a future.

Columnist Richard Reeves suggests that "the end of news" may be near. The avalanche of news about the rapid changes of modern life is turning people off. Audiences "do not want complicated and emotionally complex stories that remind them of their own frustrations and powerlessness."

Reeves is probably right about the growing avoidance of complexity. People don't want to think.

That's why simplicity has such power. By oversimplifying a complex issue, you are making it easy for people to make a decision without too much thought. Consider the complex trial of O.J. Simpson and how Johnnie Cochran put the essence of his argument into one memorable line: "If the glove doesn't fit, you must acquit."

"Make your scandals complex and you can beat the rap everytime," says speechwriter Peggy Noonan referring to Whitewater, which, unlike Watergate, lacked the easily grasped story line that people want.

But psychologist Dr. Carol Moog comes at the problem from another vantage point. She states that in our culture there's a "paranoia of omission." There's a sense that you have to cover all your options because you could be attacked at any moment. You can't miss anything or it could be fatal to your career.

In other words, if you have only one idea and that idea fails, you have no safety net. And because we are so success-driven, it magnifies the number one fear, "fear of failure."

You feel naked with a simple idea. A variety of ideas enables a person to hedge his or her bets.

Our general education and most management training teach us to deal with every variable, seek out every option, and analyze every angle. This leads to maddening complexity. And the most clever among us produce the most complex proposals and recommendations.

Unfortunately, when you start spinning out all kinds of different solutions, you're on the road to chaos. You end up with contradictory ideas and people running in different directions. Simplicity requires that you narrow the options and return to a single path.

Dr. Moog also had some interesting observations about buzzwords. To her, a management buzzword is like a movie star with whom we fall in love.

The buzzword comes with a beautiful book jacket and a dynamic speaker that has what we all love, charisma. Whether or not I understand this starlet isn't important, because I'm in love. And besides, people are afraid to question somebody who's a big shot or to challenge what they think is a big idea. (That's "fear of speaking.")

The best way to deal with these natural fears is to focus on the problem. It's analogous to how a ballet dancer avoids getting dizzy when doing a pirouette. The trick is to focus on one object in the audience every time your head comes around.

Needless to say, you have to recognize the right problem on which to focus.

If you're Volvo, the problem on which to focus is how to maintain your leadership in the concept of "safety" as others tries to jump on your idea.

That's pretty obvious.

But there are times when the problem isn't so obvious. Such was the case in recent years for Procter & Gamble, the world's preeminent marketer. You might assume that its problem was to find ways to sell more stuff.

The new management recognized the real problem. Does the world need 31 varieties of Head & Shoulders shampoo? Or 52 versions of Crest? As P&G's president, Durk Jager, said in *Business Week* magazine,[1] "It's mind-boggling how difficult we've made it for consumers over the years."

As the article put it, he and CEO John Pepper realized that after decades of spinning out new-and-improved this, lemon-freshened that, and extra-jumbo-size the other thing, P&G decided it sells too many different kinds of stuff.

This solution to that problem was simple, though implementing it was a complex process. The company standardized product formulas and reduced complex deals and coupons. Gone are 27 types of promotions, including bonus packs and outlandish tactics such as goldfish giveaways to buyers of Spic & Span. (Many froze to death during midwinter shipping.) P&G also got rid of marginal brands, cut product lines, and trimmed new product launches.

So with less to sell, sales went down, right? Wrong. In hair care alone, by slashing the number of items in half, the company increased its share by 5 points.

Our friends at P&G certainly weren't afraid of simplicity. Over the past five years they've used it to increase their business by a third.

That's the power of simplicity.

A SIMPLE SUMMATION

Complexity is not to be admired. It's to be avoided.

CHAPTER 2

Common sense

It can make things simple

You must draw on language, logic and simple common sense to determine essential issues and establish a concrete course of action.

— Abraham Lincoln

The real antidote for fear of simplicity is common sense. Unfortunately, people often leave their common sense out in the parking lot when they come to work.

As Henry Mintzberg, professor of management at McGill University, said, "Management is a curious phenomenon. It is generously paid, enormously influential and significantly devoid of common sense."[2]

Common sense is wisdom that is shared by all. It's something that registers as an obvious truth to a community.

Simple ideas tend to be obvious ideas because they have a ring of truth about them. But people distrust their instincts. They feel there must be a hidden, more complex answer. Wrong. What's obvious to you is obvious to many. That's why an obvious answer usually works so well in the marketplace.

One of the secrets of the buzzword gurus is to start with a simple, obvious idea and make it complex. A *Time* magazine commentary on a Stephen Covey book captured this phenomenon:

> His genius is for complicating the obvious, and as a result his books are graphically chaotic. Charts and diagrams bulge from the page. Sidebars and boxes chop the chapters into bite-size morsels. The prose buzzes with the cant phrases — empower, modeling, bonding, agent of change — without which his books would deflate like a blown tire. He uses more exclamation points than Gidget.[3]

If you look up the dictionary definition of "common sense," you discover that it is native good judgment that is free from emotional bias or intellectual subtlety. It's also not dependent on special technical knowledge.

In other words, you are seeing things as they really are. You are following the dictates of cold logic, eliminating both sentiment and self-interest from your decision. Nothing could be simpler.

In the prior chapter, the new management at Procter & Gamble clearly saw the world of the supermarket as it really was: confusing. And that clarity of vision led management to the simple, commonsense strategy of simplifying things.

Consider this scenario. If you were to ask 10 people at random how well a Cadillac would sell if it looked like a Chevrolet, just about all they would say is, "Not very well."

These people are using nothing but common sense in their judgment. They have no data or research to support their conclusion. They also have no technical knowledge or intellectual subtlety. To them a Cadillac is a big expensive car and a Chevrolet is a smaller inexpensive car. They are seeing things as they really are.

But at General Motors, rather than seeing the world as it is, those in charge would rather see it as they want it to be. Common sense is ignored and the Cimarron is born. Not surprisingly, it didn't sell very well. (And we're being kind.)

Was this a lesson learned? It does not appear to be so. GM is now back with the Catera, another Cadillac that looks like a Chevrolet. Like its predecessor, it probably won't sell very well because it makes no sense. You know it and I know it. GM doesn't want to know it.

Leonardo da Vinci saw the human mind as a laboratory for gathering material from the eyes, ears, and other organs of perception—material that was then channeled through the organ of common sense. In other words, common sense is a sort of supersense that rides herd over our other senses. It's supersense that many in business refuse to trust.

Maybe we should correct that. You don't have to just be in business to ignore simple common sense. Consider the complex world of economists, a group that works hard at outwitting simple common sense.

There is nothing economists enjoy more than telling the uninitiated that plain evidence of the senses is wrong. They tend to ignore the human condition and declare that people are "maximizers of utility."

In econo-talk we become "calculators of self-interest." To economists, if we all have enough information we will make rational decisions.

Anyone who's hung around the marketing world for a while realizes that people are quite irrational at times. Right now, we're overrun by four-wheel-drive vehicles designed to travel off the road. Does anybody ever leave the road? Less than 10 percent. Do people need these vehicles? Not really. Why do they buy them? Because everyone else is buying them. How's that for "rational"?

The world cannot be put into mathematical formulas. It's too irrational. It's the way it is.

Now some words about intellectual subtlety.

A company often goes wrong when it is conned with subtle research and arguments about where the world is headed. (Nobody really knows, but many make believe they know.) These views are carefully crafted and usually mixed in with some false assumptions disguised as facts.

For example, many years ago Xerox was led to believe that in the office of the future everything—phones, computers, and copiers— would be an integrated system. (Bad prediction.) To play in this world, you needed to offer everything. Thus Xerox needed to buy or build computers and other noncopier equipment to offer in this on-rushing automated world.

Xerox was told it could do this because people saw the company as a skilled, high-technology company. (This was a false assumption. People saw it as a copier company.)

Twenty years and several billion dollars later, Xerox realized that the office of the future is still out in the future. And any Xerox machine that can't make a copy is in trouble. It was a painful lesson in technical knowledge and intellectual subtlety overwhelming good judgment.

Finally, some thoughts about a business school education, which seems to submerge common sense.

By the time students finish their first year, they already have an excellent command of the words and phrases that identify them as MBA wanna-bes. They have become comfortably familiar with jargon like "risk/reward ratio", "discounted cash flow", "pushing numbers", "expected value", and so forth.

After a while, all this uncommon language overwhelms critical thought and common sense. You get the appearance of deliberation where none may exist.

Ross Perot, in a visit to the Harvard Business School, observed, "The trouble with you people is that what you call environmental scanning, I call looking out the window."

To think in simple, commonsense terms you must begin to follow these guidelines:

1. **Get your ego out of the situation.** Good judgment is based on reality. The more you screen things through your ego, the farther you get from reality.

2. **You've got to avoid wishful thinking.** We all want things to go a certain way. But how things go are often out of our control. Good common sense tends to be in tune with the way things are going.

3. **You've got to be better at listening.** Common sense by definition is based on what others think. It's thinking that is common to many. People who don't have their ears to the ground lose access to important common sense.

4. **You've got to be a little cynical.** Things are sometimes the opposite of the way they really are. That's often the case because someone is pursuing their own agenda. Good common sense is based on the experiences of many, not the wishful thinking of some.

A SIMPLE SUMMATION

Trust your common sense. It will tell you what to do.

CHAPTER 3

Complex language

It can cloud people's minds

I notice that you use plain, simple language, short words, and brief sentences. That is the way to write English. It is the modern way and the best way. Stick to it.

— Mark Twain,
In a letter to a young friend

When Shakespeare wrote Hamlet, he had 20,000 words with which to work. When Lincoln scribbled the Gettysburg Address on the back of an envelope there were about 114,000 words at his disposal. Today there are more than 600,000 words in *Webster's Dictionary*. Tom Clancy appears to have used all of them in his last thousand-page novel.

Language is getting more complicated. As a result, people have to fight off the tendency to try out some of these new and rarely used words.

What if some famous adages had been written with a heavier hand and some fancier words? Here's a sampling of some simple ideas made complex:

- Pulchritude possesses profundity of a merely cutaneous nature. *(Beauty is only skin deep.)*

- It is not efficacious to indoctrinate a superannuated canine with innovative maneuvers. *(You can't teach an old dog new tricks.)*

- Visible vapors that issue from carbonaceous materials are a harbinger of imminent conflagration. *(Where there's smoke, there's fire.)*

- A revolving mass of lithic conglomerates does not accumulate a congery of small green bryophitic plants. *(A rolling stone gathers no moss.)*

You get the point. Good writing and speech can't be confusing. They have to be clear and understandable, and the shorter the better.

Television journalist Bill Moyers had this advice for good writing: "Empty your knapsack of all adjectives, adverbs and clauses that slow your stride and weaken your pace. Travel light. Remember the most memorable sentences in the English language are also the shortest: 'The King is dead' and 'Jesus wept.'"

If all these new words aren't bad enough, business people are busy inventing their own language. Here is a direct quote from one futurist and management guru: "Managers have come to understand that there are multiple modes of change. One is what I call 'paradigm enhancement,' which the total-quality, continuous-improvement message has been all about. The other is radical change — or para-digm-shift change — which is unlike any other kind of change that you must deal with."

Fortune[4] magazine reported that Better Communications, a firm in Lexington, Massachusetts, that teaches writing skills to employers, clipped these management speak phrases from what it described as "memos from hell" circulating at Fortune 500 companies.

- Top leadership helicoptered this vision. *(The bosses are looking beyond next week.)*

- Added value is the keystone to exponentially accelerating profit curves. *(Let's grow sales and profits by offering more of what customers want.)*

- We need to dimensionalize this management initiative. *(Let's all make a plan.)*

- We utilized a concert of cross-functional expertise. *(People from different departments talked to each other.)*

- Don't impact employee incentivization programs. *(Don't screw around with people's pay.)*

- Your job, for the time being, has been designated as "retained." *(You're not fired yet.)*

Why do businesspeople talk so mysteriously about thing like core competency *(what we do well)* or empowerment *(delegating)* or para-digms *(how we do things)*? It's gotten so bad that in a book entitled *Fad*

Surfing in the Boardroom, the author had to publish a dictionary on nouveau business words and *The Wall Street Journal* (June 8, 1998) has uncovered a new sport called "buzzword bingo." Employees tally points in meetings by tracking the jargon and clichés their bosses spout. ("Deliverables", "net net" and "impactfulness all score points.)

We sense that businesspeople feel that by using these pompous words they will look as smart, complicated, and significant as possible. But all it really does is make them unintelligible.

Jack Welch, the highly successful chairman of General Electric, put it well when he said in an interview in the *Harvard Business Review*:

> "Insecure managers create complexity. Frightened, nervous managers use thick, convoluted planning books and busy slides filled with everything they've known since childhood. Real leaders don't need clutter. People must have the self-confidence to be clear, precise, to be sure that every person in their organization—highest to lowest—understands what the business is trying to achieve. But it's not easy. You can't believe how hard it is for people to be simple, how much they fear being simple. They worry that if they're simple, people will think they're simple-minded. In reality, of course, it's just the reverse. Clear, tough-minded people are the most simple.[5]"

All that said, what's a manager to do to fight off complexity? Help is available.

Dr. Rudolph Flesch staged a one-person crusade against pomposity and murkiness in writing. (Among his books is *The Art of Plain Talk.*) He was one of the first to suggest that people in business who write like they talk will write better.

Flesch's approach would work like this in responding to a letter: "Thanks for your suggestion, Jack. I'll think about it and get back to you as soon as I can." The opposite of his approach would be: "Your suggestion has been received this date, and after due and careful deliberations, we shall report our findings to you."

Others have discovered that you can actually measure simplicity in writing. In the 1950s, Robert Gunning created the *Gunning Fog Index,* which shows how easy something is to read in terms of the number of words and their difficulty, the number of complete thoughts, and the average sentence length in a piece of copy.

You can win the fight against fog by adhering to 10 principles of clear writing.

1. Keep sentences short.

2. Pick the simple word over the complex word.

3. Choose the familiar word.

4. Avoid unnecessary words.

5. Put action in your verbs.

6. Write like you talk.

7. Use terms your readers can picture.

8. Tie in with your reader's experience. *(The essence of positioning.)*

9. Make full use of variety.

10. Write to express, not impress.

You have to encourage simple, direct language and ban business buzz-words not only in writing but also in talking.

But more than that, you have to encourage simplicity as the way to better listening. Overwhelmed by the incessant babble of the modern world, the skill of listening has fallen on hard times. Studies show that people recall only 20 percent of what they heard in the past few days.

In a July 10, 1997 article, the *Wall Street Journal* reported that we've become a nation of blabbermouths who aren't listening at all. We're just waiting for our chance to talk.

And if all this weren't bad enough, the newspaper reports, biology also works against attentive listening. Most people speak at a rate of 120 to 150 words a minute, but the human brain can easily process 500 words a minute leaving plenty of time for mental fidgeting. If a speaker is the least bit complex and confusing, it takes a heroic effort to stay tuned in instead of faking it.

Meetings and presentations that aren't simple and to the point are a waste of time and money. Little will be communicated as people simply dial out. This can be very costly.

Many years ago, an associate and I were leaving a two-hour meeting where a design firm had presented its recommendations in a multimillion dollar logo design project. As usual, the presenters used terms such as "modality" and " paradigms" and threw in vague references to "color preference." It was a presentation loaded with obscure and complex concepts. Because of my low rank, I admitted to my fellow worker that I was quite confused by what was said and was asking for his overview. He suddenly smiled and looked quite relieved. He then went on to admit that he hadn't understood a word that was said but was afraid to admit it so as to appear stupid.

That company wasted millions of dollars changing a perfectly good logo because no one in the meeting had the courage to ask the presenters to explain their recommendations in simple, understandable language. If they had, they and their logos would have been laughed out of the room.

The moral of this story is that you should never let a confusing word or concept go unchallenged. If you do, some expensive mistakes can be made. Tell presenters to translate their complex terms into simple language. Never be afraid to say, "I don't get it." You have to be intolerant of intellectual arrogance.

Don't be suspicious of your first impressions. Your first impressions are often the most accurate.

Don't fight the feeling of looking foolish. In some ways the most naïve-sounding questions can turn out to be most profound.

Let's give Peter Drucker the last words on simple language.

"One of the most degenerate tendencies of the last forty years is the belief that if you are understandable, you are vulgar. When I was growing up, it was taken for granted that economists, physicists, psychologists — leaders in any discipline — would make themselves understood. Einstein spent years with three different collaborators to make his theory of relativity accessible to the layman. Even John Maynard Keynes tried hard to make his economics accessible.

But just the other day, I heard a senior scholar seriously reject a younger colleague's work because more than five people could understand what he's doing. Literally.

We cannot afford such arrogance. Knowledge is power, which is why people who had it in the past often tried to make a secret of it. In post-capitalism, power comes from transmitting information to make it productive, not from hiding it."

A SIMPLE SUMMATION

Big ideas almost always come in small words.

Management Issues

How to cope with complexities while bringing a degree of order and consistency to complex enterprises

CHAPTER 4

Information

Too much can confuse you

The art of being wise is the art of knowing what to overlook.

> — William James
> American psychologist and philosopher

Business complexity is fed by the ever-increasing amount of information that is being piped into the business world in as many ways as Silicon Valley can invent. There's no escaping what David Shenk described in his book *Data Smog*, the "noxious muck and druck of the information age."

Currently, information processing accounts for half the gross national product. A lot of it ends up on paper that someone has to read. The following statistic might threaten you, but today business managers are expected to read one million words per week. (Can you afford the time to read this?)

The information age began with the first computer, which was about the size of a living room. Today we have more powerful machines that are lap tops, palm tops, finger tops—you name it. And they're all out there spitting out information that we feel isn't helping matters.

Peter Drucker agrees. "Computers," he says, "may have done more harm than good by making managers even more inwardly focused. Executives are so enchanted by the internal data the computer generates—and that's all it generates so far, by and large—they have neither the mind nor the time for the outside. Yet results are only on the outside. I find more and more executives less and less well informed (about the outside world)."[6]

It's no wonder that *USA Today* did an article entitled "Boomer Brain Meltdown" that described how this generation faces more frequent memory lapses.

Some in this article believe that it's not age that is the main cause of memory loss. It's information overload. Their premise is that our minds are like the memory of a computer and our disks are full.

Consider numbers. In years gone by all you needed to remember were your telephone number and your address. Today, it's burglar alarm codes, a social security number, e-mail numbers, fax numbers, calling card numbers, and PINS for ATMs. The digits are crowding out the words.

Some people even believe that information overload will become a medical problem. Len Riggio, CEO of Barnes & Noble, predicts that in the 21st century, people will be popping pills to help empty their minds. "Losing thoughts and forgetting will be the equivalent of shedding pounds and dieting," says Mr. Riggio.

We have some less drastic suggestions to reduce information right now, if you want your mind to operate at maximum efficiency and speed.

Here's how to fight through the fog while still trying to see what's happening.

The first challenge is to acknowledge that you can't absorb everything you think you need to know. Once you master that mental hurdle, things get easier. You'll be able to prioritize, delegate, and just let things slide. (You don't have to answer or even read everything that comes to you.) The very idea of actively eliminating information is a taboo for some. But what sounds like censorship is, in fact, self-preservation.

As you limit content, you'll learn to savor it more. Be ruthless as you hack your way through all the noise. Clear the decks for the important stuff.

Get started by spending two hours deciding what sources of information and intelligence are critical for you and your business. What newsletters and periodicals are "must" reads? What distribution lists must your name be on? What web sites must be bookmarked? What associations must you belong to?

Boil it all down to the highest-quality stuff and read that first. Cancel or get rid of what's only marginal.

And when you're the one doing the communicating, be more economical in everything you write, publish, broadcast, or post online.

You're supposed to be a decision maker, not an information expert.

Let's say you need to know something. If you (or your assistant or your secretary) can't find a complete answer in 15 minutes or less, you're better off asking a professional researcher or research firm to do the job. One good choice: Find/SVP, with offices in the U.S. and 32 other countries.

If you're blessed with an assistant, have him or her select and highlight the stuff you need to see from newsmagazines or "survey journals" in your field that abstract stories and articles. This will help you cut through all the blather.

COR Healthcare Resources is an excellent example of a company that publishes abstracts of articles. Each month it scans thousands of articles in 150 publications in order to produce a dozen different newsletters with titles like *Healthcare Marketing Abstracts and Healthcare Leadership Review.*

COR's founder, Dean Anderson, says, "The newsletters appear to be just digests of articles. But their value depends just as much on what we leave out as what we put in. The goal is to simplify the complex healthcare industry into an understandable framework. We're strong believers that once complexity is reduced, uncertainty is minimized, and decision-makers can start to take charge of their jobs and their lives."

If you can't get a story synopsis, start with the table of contents of pertinent magazines. Scan for topics and article summaries. Decide what you want to read now, tear out for reading later, or save.

As you read an article, underline or highlight anything you want to refer to later. If there's no underlining or highlighting when you finish, toss the article.

Keep a folder of "looks interesting" or "want to read" articles or mailings. They're good for plane rides.

Challenge every piece of paper to show you why you shouldn't throw it out. If it meets the challenge, act on it, place it in a to-do stack, send it someone, or file it.

Demand that any report that reaches you have a one-paragraph or one-page summary. If it doesn't, send it back.

Each Friday, ask your direct reports to tell you in a single page what important things happened during the week and what they mean for your business.

E-mail's greatest virtue is that it's cheap. That's also its biggest danger.

E-mail was supposed to move us closer to the paperless office. Instead, it seems to have replaced cogent, carefully written memos with electronic drivel that captures a mental puff every 60 seconds. (A Gallup Poll in May 1998 found that a typical office worker sends and receives an average of 60 e-mails a day.

Before you know it, you'll be getting hundreds of e-mails a day from your staff, your friends, your relatives, your business contacts, your suppliers, your clients.

Decide whether you'll actually open and read e-mail by what's in the header. Scan by sender and subject. Give messages from your clients and the boss priority.

Look for filters in your e-mail package. Filters let you prioritize messages from key people and separate them from other stuff.

Lighten your load in the first place. Don't put your e-mail address on your business cards. Give it only to people who need it.

Open e-mail only at set times—perhaps when you start work or at the end of the day. The whole point of e-mail is that the other person doesn't know when or even if you looked at it. If your computer constantly flags incoming mail, and if you constantly reply, the little buggers just multiply.

Send brief responses. Scold people who write long e-mails or leave long voice mails.

Ask friends not to forward trivia, chatter, jokes, and other junk.

If you just need to get facts straight or solicit opinions, use e-mail or fax. Don't call a meeting unless you have brainstorming to do or want to iron out a group problem.

Be careful about the seductive software for presentation graphics. It can turn very simple thoughts into very complex images.

When you're presenting information on a screen, keep it simple. Seven lines of text is the limit. One visual per slide is the ideal.

Have you tried video conferencing instead of a traditional meeting? You should. The pictures and sound are much improved.

Give the folks at PictureTel a call (unless you fancy flying into Grand Rapids in February for a meeting).

An engineering VP for a broadcasting company provided this snapshot of business life circa 1998: "I would start the morning with 40 e-mail messages, the phone ringing off the hook, the fax going, and that's on the few days I was in my office and not on the road."

Our beleaguered executive is armed with the personal technologies that busy people lug around: cell phone, notebook computer, two-way pager, and portable printer.

Does all this gear make life simpler? Make the executive more productive? More efficient? Are you kidding!

Professor Hugh Heclo of George Mason University observes: "In the long run, excesses of technology mean that the comparative advantage shifts from those with information glut to those with ordered knowledge, from those who can process vast amounts of throughput to those who can explain what is worth knowing, and why."

So as you fight through the smog, remember:

1. There is a difference between data and information.
2. You can get addicted to your favorite communications device.
3. Don't be a pack rat. You can retrieve anything electronically.
4. Most requests are not as urgent as the sender believes.
5. Always separate urgent messages from nonurgent ones.
6. Always respond briefly and to the point. Don't add more noise than signal.

A SIMPLE SUMMATION

If you unclutter your mind, you'll think more clearly.

CHAPTER 5

Consultants

The source of a lot of nonsense

There are about 700 business schools in the U.S. alone. All these institutions are full of academics desperate to make their name as management theorists.

> — Robert Lenzer and Stephen S. Johnson
> *Forbes*

In the beginning there was Peter Drucker, quietly dishing out sound management advice. As Intel's Andy Grove put it, "Drucker is a hero of mine. He writes and thinks with exquisite clarity—a standout among a bunch of muddled fad mongers."

Then in the 1980s Tom Peters exploded on the scene with his book about excellence. That was the dawning of an era of Tom Peters wanna-bes whom one could safely call modern-day Robin Hoods. They rob from the rich and keep it. But instead of bows and arrows, this crowd is armed with complex buzzwords and ideas that they use to nail their prey.

An article in *Fortune* magazine entitled "In Search of Suckers" put it quite accurately: "Quietly, without fanfare, the advice business has been hijacked. New gurus armed with nothing more than pens, podiums and tremendous shamelessness have co-opted what used to be a nice, wholesome calling: dishing out good advice to business men and women."[7]

Rupert Murdoch was a little more blunt when he was asked whether there was any management guru that he followed or admired. His response, "Guru? You find a gem here or there. But most of it's fairly obvious, you know. You go to the bookstore business section and you see all these wonderful titles and you spend $300 and then you throw them all away."[8]

As even Tom Peters admits, "We're the only society that believes it can keep getting better and better. So we keep on getting suckered in by people like me."[9]

Much has been written about the good, the bad, and the ugly of consultancy.

You should realize that complexity is at the heart of a bad consultant's business. Their view of such a consultant, and it may be an accurate one, is that companies won't pay a lot for simplicity. In fact, it would sometimes appear that the less a company understands about the process, the more it will pay.

If it were simple, companies would do it themselves.

So the trick is to constantly invent new complex concepts. For example, most companies can understand competing in the marketplace. So in an article in the *McKinsey Quarterly Magazine*,[10] readers are told that there are now two worlds in which to compete: the marketplace and a new one called "marketspace." (Nice, it even rhymes.) All this is about creating digital assets, a concept that causes the eyes of a 60-year-old CEO to begin to glaze over.

Then, to introduce a little terror into the equation, the reader is warned that "old business axioms no longer apply" and companies "must oversee a physical value chain, but must also build and exploit a virtual value chain."

What the authors are hoping for is the following reader response: "Quick, get me the phone number of those two Harvard guys who wrote the article I don't understand. We could be in trouble."

We're not saying all this information is bad, but it's tough enough for that CEO to figure out how to survive in the "marketplace," let alone a new thing called the "marketspace."

What we really get a chuckle out of is when the consultants start to sue each other over their complex concepts. Such was the case of a consulting company called Stern Stewart that came up with a hot financial concept called "economic value added," or EVA. (The company even trademarked it.) KPMG, another large consultant, decided to launch its own version called "economic value management," or EVM. Enter the lawyers and the lawsuits and a great deal of mud slinging. Chaos has broken out in the land of Robin Hood. The merry men are shooting arrows at each other instead of the rich.

But what really generate the most nonsense are those wonderful charts and graphs that are created to explain the process for which you are shelling out big bucks. Consider the following chart that was

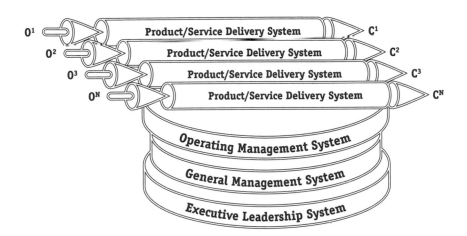

designed to explain the "high performance organization." It sure does look lethal. (Believe it or not, this is real.)

In fact, this looks so dangerous that the company that adopts this will probably explode in six months or so.

Now, let's say you're a consultant that wants to develop a process where you could address strategic questions for a decade of big billing. The trick is to slow down the final decision that would end the project. Best we can figure out, the following process gives you that kind of slow motion.

As you work your way through this maze, you can "decide direction" or "change direction." You can move into "alternatives" or double

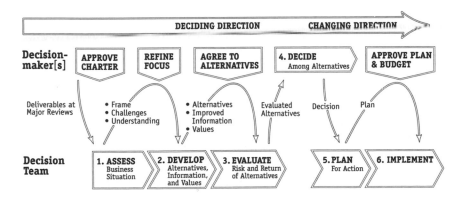

back and "refine focus." And each little wiggle is worth a lot of billable time.

Thinking just doesn't have to be that complicated unless you're trying to make it that complicated.

Maybe the answer to improving company performance comes down to introducing simple ideas into a company and making sure they get done. Consider the approach of GE's Jack Welch, arguably one of America's most successful CEOs.

His management mantras are pretty simple. First, you tell your people that you believe in being number one or number two in a field. If not, they run the risk of being sold. And Mr. Welch did what he promised as he earned the nickname of "Neutron Jack." The buildings were there but the people were gone.

Next it was the "boundaryless" sharing of ideas, a process that breaks down corporate hierarchies to make sure that information flows up and down.

Now he's pushing a defect-reduction program called Six Sigma. The goal of the program is to reduce defects to the point where errors are almost nonexistent. The benefits: happy customers and big cost savings.

As *Forbes* magazine wrote, "the secret of Jack Welch's success is not a series of brilliant insights or bold gambles but a fanatical attention to detail."

Don't get us wrong. Good consultants bring that vital thing called "objectivity" to the equation. They have experience and a perspective on things that insiders sometimes lack. But, most importantly, they are outsiders.

Insiders aren't lacking in answers. Often companies could have saved a lot of money by turning to employees instead of outsiders. Why do so many companies fail to capitalize on their employees' knowledge?

One reason is that familiarity breeds contempt. Many executives see nothing but imperfections and mistakes in their employees. By contrast, consultants aren't around long enough for their blemishes to become noticeable.

There's also the issue of compromise. A good consultant has to search for what is right in the context of what a company can or cannot do. It has nothing to do with buzzwords or fancy processes.

Let's return to one of our heroes, Peter Drucker, to get his view on what a good consultant is about:

> "I was taught this when I started in 1944 on my first big consulting assignment, a study of the management structure and management policies of the General Motors Corporation. Alfred P. Sloan, Jr., who was then chairman and chief executive officer of the company, called me to his office at the start of my study and said: "I shall not tell you what to study, what to write, or what conclusions to come to. This is your task. My only instruction to you is to put down what you think is right as you see it. Don't you worry about our reaction. Don't you worry about whether we will like this or dislike that. And don't you, above all, concern yourself with the compromises that might be needed to make your recommendations acceptable. There is not one executive in this company who does not know how to make every single conceivable compromise without any help from you. But he can't make the right compromise unless you first tell him what 'right' is."[11]

It's all about doing the right thing—not the fashionable thing.

And consider this. The consultants themselves admit their shortcomings. A Bain & Company survey in 1997 showed that 77 percent of 4,000 executives surveyed said that the management tools they bought promised more than they delivered, and that there was no correlation to financial success.

So before you leap, you might want to consider the following criticisms of most management theories:

1. They degenerate into fads because they are only quick fixes for a topical problem.

2. Information on success rates is seldom available.

3. They waste energy and resources. The company sends hundreds of executives off to seminars and hires newly minted consultants to spread the gospel.

4. They create unrealistic expectations.

5. They undermine the confidence of employees, who greet each new buzzword with increasing skepticism.

If this doesn't give you pause, then we wish you good luck!

A SIMPLE SUMMATION

Never trust anyone you don't understand.

CHAPTER 6

Competitors

Simply think of them as the enemy

Everything is very simple in war, but the simplest thing is difficult.

— Karl von Clausewitz
Famous military historian

Business today is not about reengineering or continuous improvement. Business is about war.

We first presented this observation more than 25 years ago in a book entitled *Marketing Warfare*. In hindsight, this book was published in the dark ages of competition. A decade ago, the term "global economy" didn't exist. The vast array of technology that we take for granted was still a glimmer in the eyes of some Silicon Valley engineers. Global commerce was pretty much limited to a handful of multinational companies.

As we approach the end of this century, of the world's 100 largest economies, 51 are not countries but corporations. The 500 largest account for a stunning 70 percent of world trade.

Today's marketplace makes the one we first wrote about look like a tea party. The wars are escalating and breaking out in every part of the globe. Everyone is after everyone's business everywhere.

All this means that the principles of *Marketing Warfare* are more important than ever. Companies must learn how to deal with their competitors—how to avoid their strengths and how to exploit their weaknesses. Organizations must learn that it's not about do or die for your company. It's about making the other guy die for his company.

In simplest terms, to be successful today a company must become competitor-oriented. It must look for weak points in the positions of its competitors and then launch marketing attacks against those weak points.

It's all about pursuing the right competitive strategy. It's all about understanding the four types of marketing warfare and figuring out which applies to your situation.

The strategic square

Defensive Warfare	**Offensive Warfare**
Flanking Warfare	**Guerrilla Warfare**

These principles constitute a very simple strategic model for company survival in the twenty-first century. Let's review and update them.

1. Defensive Warfare Is What Market Leaders Wage. Leadership is reserved for those companies whose customers perceive them as the leader. (Not pretenders to be leaders.)

Your most aggressive leaders are willing to attack themselves with new ideas. We have long used Gillette as a classic defender. Every two or three years it replaces its existing blade with a new idea. We've had two-bladed razors (Trac-II). We've had adjustable two-bladed razors (Atra). We've had shock-absorbent razors(Sensor). And now we have three-bladed razors (Mach 3). A rolling company gathers no competitors.

An aggressive leader always blocks competitive moves. When Bic introduced the disposable razor, Gillette quickly countered with the twin-bladed disposable (Good News). It now dominates this category.

All this adds up to over 60 percent of the blade market. That's a leader.

2. Offensive Warfare Is the Strategy for the Number Two or Three in a Category. The first principle is to avoid the strength of a leader's position. What you want to do is find a weakness and attack at that point. Then you focus all your efforts at that point.

In recent years, the fastest-growing pizza chain in America is Papa John's Pizza. Papa John's attacked Pizza Hut at its weak point, ingredients. John Schnatter, the founder, got his hands on the best tomato sauce in the country. It was a sauce that the other chains couldn't buy. This became the cornerstone of his concept, "Better Ingredients. Better Pizza."

John has stayed narrowly focused on the better ingredients concept in everything he does such as cheese and toppings. He even filters the water for better dough.

As the *Wall Street Journal* reported, "Papa John's is on a tear." This is not the kind of news that Pizza Hut is very happy about.

One of the best ways of attacking a leader is with a new-generation technology.

In the land of paper making, quality control systems have become a two-horse race between Measurex, the current leader, and AccuRay (a part of ABB), the former leader of systems that measure paper's uniformity as it is produced.

AccuRay has just attacked Measurex with a new generation of electronic scanning that measures the entire sheet instead of just parts of the sheet. This new weapon is called Hyper Scan Full Sheet Imaging, and it promises a quality control measurement that Measurex can't measure up to. This idea will work because AccuRay just made its competitor obsolete.

3. Smaller or New Players That Are Trying to Get a Foothold in a Category by Avoiding the Main Battle Pursue Flanking Warfare. This strategy usually involves a move into an uncontested area and contains the element of surprise.

Often it's a new idea such as gourmet popping corn (Orville Redenbacher) or Dijon mustard (Grey Poupon). Sometimes it's an old idea that suddenly catches on, such as four-wheel drive vehicles (Jeep).

A brilliant flanking move has been under way in the golf world. While others have focused on drivers, irons, and putters, Adams Golf has gone into an area that has never been heavily contested. (It lies in the fairway about 200 yards from the green.)

Adams's flanking move was to introduce a patented flat design of fairway woods that were perfect for those tight lies. The simple but brilliant product name says it all: Tight Lies Fairway Woods. Very quickly, they have become the fastest-growing fairway woods in the country.

When a 19-year-old named Michael Dell started his own little computer company, he knew he couldn't compete with established companies for floor space in stores. However, the rules of the industry, at that time, dictated that computers had to be sold in stores. Every company in the industry believed that customers wouldn't trust a mail-order company to provide such a high-end item.

Michael Dell broke the rule. He flanked the industry and direct-marketed. And he built an $800 million company in five years.

4. Guerrilla Warfare Is Often the Land of the Smaller Companies. The first principle is that of finding a market small enough to defend. It's the big fish in the small pond strategy.

No matter how successful you become, never act like a leader. Going "big time" is what does in successful guerrilla companies. (Anyone remember People's Express Airlines?)

Finally, you have to be prepared to bug out at a moment's notice. Small companies can't afford to take those losses. Melt into the jungle so you can live to fight another day.

One of the most interesting guerrilla case studies is under way down in the Caribbean. This is where the tourism wars are being waged by all the islands, big and small.

Grenada is one of the southernmost islands in the Caribbean. Famous for President Reagan's invasion to exit a few Cubans, Grenada is now trying to get a share of the tourist business.

Because it's late in the game, the island is unspoiled. There is little concrete, and there are no overdeveloped beaches. In fact there are no buildings higher than a palm tree. That has enabled them to develop a strategy of being the unspoiled island or the "Caribbean the way it used to be."

This is a "defensible" idea since all the other islands are developed. There's no way they can suddenly become unspoiled.

But smaller jungle fighters must beware of the fact that the jungle can become an overpopulated place. Such is the case with microbrews, recently the successful guerrillas in the beer wars, whose numbers have jumped fourfold, to 1306, since 1993, according to the Institute for Brewing Studies.

Tantalized by consumer fancy for every imaginable new concoction, and with easy access to capital, micros churned out as many as 4000 different brands. With that many guerrillas in a small market, you end up just killing off each other, which is just what is happening.

After meteoric growth of about 50 percent a year in 1994 and 1995, the microbrew industry has gone about as flat as day-old beer. Now, a full-fledged shakeout is on tap among brewers and brewpubs.

Who will survive the pub brawl? Many industry execs speculate that among the survivors will be Sam Adams, the only micro with a truly national franchise, and long-time California micros Sierra Nevada and Anchor Steam.

Finally, if you're at war, it's important that you adopt the qualities of a good general.

- **You must be flexible.** You must be flexible to adjust the strategy to the situation and not vice versa. A good general has built-in biases, but he or she will seriously consider all alternatives and points of view before making a decision.

- **You must have mental courage.** At a point in time, your open mind has to close and a decision must be made. A good general reaches deep inside to find the strength of will and mental courage to prevail.

- **You must be bold.** When the time is right, you must strike quickly and decisively. Boldness is an especially valuable trait when the tide is running with you. That's when to pour it on.

Beware of those that exhibit too much courage when the deck is stacked against them.

- **You must know the facts.** A good general builds strategy from the ground up, starting with the details. When the strategy is developed, it will be simple but powerful.

- **You need to be lucky.** Luck can play a large part in any success, provided you can exploit it. And when your luck runs out, you ought to be prepared to cut your losses quickly. "Capitulation is not a disgrace," says Clausewitz. "A general can no more entertain the idea of fighting to the last man than a good chess player would play an obviously lost game."

A SIMPLE SUMMATION

Know thy competitors.
Avoid their strength.
Exploit their weakness.

CHAPTER 7

Strategy

It's all about differentiation

In real estate it's location, location, location.
In business it's differentiate, differentiate, differentiate.

> — Robert Goizueta,
> former Coca-Cola CEO

Unfortunately, the concept of "strategy" has become quite confused thanks to gurus like Harvard's Michael Porter. In his 1985 work, *Competitive Advantage,* Porter outlines generic strategies that firms could take. But before they can pick one, things get very complex. They have to analyze the five competitive forces (potential entrants, buyers, suppliers, substitutes, and competitors), and then figure out what kind of industry they are part of (growing, declining, ripening, mature, etc.). In addition, a company should think of itself not as a single unit but as a "value chain" of "discrete activities." (Give us a break.)

Underneath all Porter's lists and copious examples is a simple truth: In a world where everyone is after your business you must supply your customers with a reason to buy you instead of your competitor. If you don't offer that reason, then you had better offer a very good price.

That reason is then packaged into a simple word or set of words that is positioned in the ultimate battleground, the minds of your customers and prospects. We call that "positioning."

It must be simple because minds hate complexity. It becomes a competitive mental angle (more on this in Chapter 15).

Unfortunately, what many companies end up with are not differentiating ideas, but meaningless slogans. Consider the following.

- Does "Solutions for a small planet" differentiate IBM? Not really. What makes IBM better than its smaller competitors is its ability to put all the pieces together. "Integrated computing" is what it does best. As Lou Gerstner puts it, "Our ability to integrate is a unique asset of this company." Now just get it in the ads, Lou.

- Does "Just do it" or "I can" differentiate Nike? Not really. What Nike has going for it more than any other manufacturer is that

Nike is "what the best athletes in the world wear." And it has Michael Jordan to prove it.

- Does "The difference is Merrill Lynch" make Merrill Lynch different? Not really. What makes it different is the depth of resources it has compared with other investment companies. "More resources. Better answers" would turn its bigness into goodness.

- Does "It's all within your reach" separate AT&T from MCI, Sprint, or other telecom companies? Not really. What would do the trick is for AT&T to focus on the concept of "reliability." That's its obvious differentiating idea. And it has the network to back up that claim.

- Do the frogs separate Budweiser from other beers? Again, not really. What does the job is telling of the long heritage behind the Budweiser brand. Kill the frogs, Mr. Busch.

Differentiating yourself comes in three parts:

1. Having a simple idea that separates you from your competition.
2. Having the credentials or the product that makes this concept real and believable.
3. Building a program to make your customers and prospects aware of this difference.

It's that simple.

Many companies know what makes them different, but it's too obvious for them to see things clearly. It's almost too simple to recognize.

If you travel down to Buenos Aires, you'll quickly discover that Quilmes is the big beer in Argentina. It enjoys about 60 percent of the market. And it has been brewing beer there since 1890.

Its advertising features a lot of great-looking gals meeting great-looking guys with the slogan "The taste of the meeting." What the company should be promoting is a simple idea that makes it unique, "Since 1890 the beer of Argentina." That's what the company is.

If you travel out West, you'll notice one of the great old brand names in America, Wells Fargo Bank. This organization goes back to 1852 when it featured the pony express and those galloping stagecoaches.

Today, those stagecoaches travel at the speed of light, thanks to computer network technology. But the essence of what makes Wells Fargo different is still the same. It could be expressed as "Fast then. Fast now." That's what it is.

Pontiac is currently running an old differentiating idea that has been successfully brought back. The concept is "wide track," and Pontiac is brilliantly dramatizing it with the simple idea that "Wider is better."

The more things change, the more things stay the same. Powerful differentiating ideas are forever. They just need upgrading from time to time. What they don't need is changing. (Coke never should have stopped using "The Real Thing.")

This kind of thinking isn't reserved for giant companies. Consider the story of Aron Streit Inc., the last independent matzo company. (For those who aren't sure, a matzo is the authentic, unleavened, unsalted and un-everything else bread that kept the Israelites alive on their flight from Egypt.)

Even though the company has only a small share of a market dominated by B. Manischewitz, the Streit's Matzo folks realize that "tradition" is just about all that distinguishes one matzo from another. Despite all the trendy outsourcing for many of its other products, Streit's still makes its matzos on Rivington Street in lower Manhattan— the same place the company has made them since 1914.

If you go to Streit's web site, you'll discover that the company knows what the difference is all about. Here's how Streit's puts it:

> Why is Streit's Matzo different from other domestic matzo brands?
> Because Streit's bakes only Streit's Matzo in our own ovens.

That's tradition and differentiation.

Zane's Cycles is the largest single-location bicycle dealer in Connecticut. How does 33-year-old Chris Zane keep sales growing 25 percent a year in a hotly competitive business?

He differentiates. He explains: "The strategy I'm best known for is my lifetime service guarantee. When a customer buys from me, if the bicycle ever fails or needs maintenance, we will do whatever it takes to get the customer back on the road. Free."

His lifetime guarantee isn't as expensive as it sounds. First, his mechanics know they're going to service the bike free as long as the customer owns it. So they tend to properly assemble each new bike the first time.

Second, the lifetime guarantee keeps the best customers coming back (the biking enthusiasts who ride often enough to require periodic service). That helps business because each service visit is the chance to see new items and thus a new selling opportunity.

What does all this mean for those strategic plans that people produce? The problem we find in most plans is that they are long on "what to do" and short on the "how to do it." There's little value in someone producing a document about increasing our share of this market or penetrating that market without that vital "How are we going to do it?" (If any plan lands on your desk without the "How," send it back.)

This is where those expensive consultants often fall down. Differentiation is not something they understand because we're dealing with perceptions.

And where they really fall down is telling a client something the client doesn't want to hear about being different. Such was the case for a big ketchup brand in Venezuela called Pampero.

By the time we were called in, Del Monte and Heinz had nudged it from its number one position. Pampero was in a decline. What was needed was a differentiating quality idea beyond its current claims of "redder" or "better."

Why is it better? What do you do to your tomatoes? After some prodding, what emerged was the fact that Pampero removes the skin so as to enhance the flavor and color. It was something their big competitors did not do.

Now that's an interesting idea, as many are aware that most recipes using whole tomatoes call for removing the skin. Pampero could exploit this "without the skins" perception of quality and taste.

When we told them that this was the best and only way to rebuild its brand's perception, Pampero became very upset. It seems the company was in the midst of changing to a money saving automated process that didn't remove the skins (a la Del Monte and Heinz). Pampero didn't want to hear about doing things the old-fashioned way.

Our recommendation was to stop the modernization plans, as "skins off" was the differentiating idea. Doing things like your bigger competitors is how to get killed in the wars out there.

Many years ago, Rosser Reeves wrote a landmark book called *Reality in Advertising.* In it he coined the term "unique selling proposition," or USP. This was something you looked for in your efforts to differentiate your product.

Today, many advertising people feel that these USPs rarely exist anymore. Products tend to be similar. So they present their clients with advertising strategy that entertains rather than differentiates. (Entertainment is good if you're selling tickets, not products.)

What these ad people don't realize is that differentiation comes in many forms. You can certainly do it in terms of product attributes. (Volvo: Drive safely.) Or you can do it by preference. (Tylenol: Pain reliever hospitals use the most.) Heritage is always good. (Stolichnaya: The Russian vodka.) Reliability is a reliable way. (Maytag. The lonely repairman.) Being first is different. (Coke: The real thing.) Convenience is always a winner. (Fresh Express: Pre-packaged lettuce.) Being first in sales is the simplest, easiest-and most direct way to say you're better. (Toyota: The best selling car in America.)

Even being different can be a difference. The National Aquarium in baltimore was faced with the "been there, done that" problem. Their strategy was to reposition the Aquarium from perceptions of fish in tanks exhibit to that of a dynamic everchanging aquatic wonderland. Their very successful strategy was very simply expressed: There's always something new at the Aquarium.

Where there's a will, there's a way to differentiate your company or product or aquarium.

A SIMPLE SUMMATION

If you're not different, you'd better have a low price.

CHAPTER 8

Customer orientation

It's a given, not a difference

Customers are not always right. They're wrong as often as they're right.

— Harold Geneen,
Former ITT chairman

Gurus and academics have made a cottage industry about customer orientation. They publish endless diatribes on how to dazzle, love, and partner with or just hang onto that person called a customer.

We are told the customer is always right, sometimes right, or usually wrong. The customer is the CEO; the customer is king; the customer is a butterfly (don't even ask).

Today we have tracts on:

- How to use customer feedback (every complaint is a gift)
- How to keep customers for life (better aftermarketing)
- How to be inspired by customers (look backward through the telescope)
- How to handle tough customers (go the extra mile)
- How to prepare for the age of the never-satisfied customer (manage in real time)

Some of this thinking can get very complex. Just consider the following:

Customer Differentiation Matrix

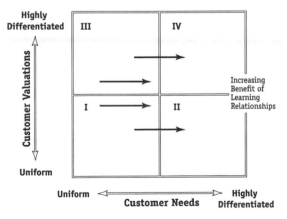

These kinds of charts are enough to drive you into the not-for-profit world.

The great myth of marketing is that "serving the customer" is the name of the game.

Many marketing people live in a dream world. They believe in the fantasy of the virgin market. This is the belief that marketing is a two-player game involving just the company and the customer. In this fantasy, a company develops a product or service designed to appeal to consumer needs and wants and then uses marketing to harvest the crop.

But there are no virgin markets. The reality of marketing is that a market consists of consumers strongly or weakly held by a range of competitors. A marketing campaign consists, therefore, of holding onto your customers while at the same time attempting to take customers away from your competitors.

What about a new product? Surely there is a lot of virgin territory when you introduce a new product.

Not true. What was the market for videocassette recorders before Sony introduced the Betamax? Zero. Of course, Sony defined its potential market as the owners of television sets, but there was no guarantee that any of them would buy a VCR.

In spite of all the talk about appealing to the needs and wants of the virgin market, most marketers would rather launch products aimed at existing markets and against entrenched competitors.

That's why many companies talk about being customer oriented. Remember the mission statements? Out of 300 companies, 211 mentioned "customers" in their statements.

George Fisher, former CEO of Eastman Kodak, had this to say. "The most important management lesson I have learned in the last 25 years is that success is driven not so much by technology or one idea, but by the people. A good company is driven by the needs and desires of customers, which are met by a well-trained, well-focused and creative workforce."

George, your problem is that you're not fulfilling the needs of your customers, especially the professional photographers. By alienating this group, Kodak lost 25 share points to Fuji Film over the past decade. That's not smart, as these people are heavy users with big mouths. (Luckily, Kodak is winning these folks back with a real differentiating idea: a new high speed, low light film.)

One can safely say that, using a poker analogy, being customer-oriented is just "openers." It gets you in the game. It certainly will not set you apart from your competitors who have read the same books and taken the same courses—some of whom, as in Fuji's case, had lower prices and superior technology.

Consider the problems of Mazda and its fuzzy undifferentiated image. Agency after agency comes in and tries its hand at the wheel.

CEO Richard Beattie gave the latest agency this directive, "We want to be a brand that appeals to people who love to drive." What kind of differentiating idea is that? How many people who don't like to drive buy cars? What about Volkswagen, which says, "Drivers wanted"? What about BMW, which offers "the Ultimate Driving Machine"? Or Mitsubishi, that proclaims "wake up and drive." (Now there's a safe idea.)

Undaunted, the new agency determined that the "brand promise" of Mazda ought to focus on the emotional desire of driving that agency referred to as "psychic refreshment." (Now there's a complex customer-oriented thought.)

All this wonderful psychology resulted in the concept, "Get in. Be moved." (If I've just spent $25,000, it better move me.) That kind of fuzzy customer oriented thinking won't move many Mazdas out of the showroom.

Focus too hard on a customer and you can see things in such complex terms that it will be impossible to figure out what to say to a customer. Consider the following chart that a consultant uses to demonstrate how to satisfy a customer's feelings.

If your marketing problem has five features, three benefits, and

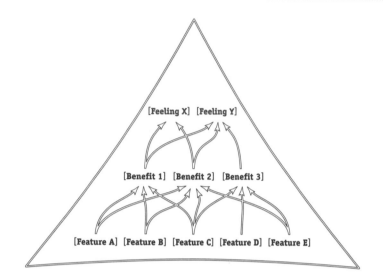

two feelings, you might want to sell the business and let someone else figure it out.

Another tricky aspect of customer orientation is the psychological fact that people tend to buy what others buy. It's called the "herd effect." (See The New Positioning, Chapter 4) This implies that you can impress your customers more by telling them about your product's popularity rather than telling them about your product.

All too often, companies try to impress prospects with a dazzling array of complexity rather than sell the simple ideas they want to buy.

Consider the Apple Newton Message Pad. It had scheduling, an address book, word processing, a calculator, spreadsheets, computer and printer part connections, a modem, infrared transmission, a built in voice recorder, e-mail, fax, and an Internet browser.

This array didn't impress customers. They were bewildered. It's no wonder it was R.I.P. Newton.

Now there are times when customer orientation can make a difference. It's when you make "service" your differentiating idea. Such is the case of Nordstrom. At a time when service was disappearing from the world of department stores, Nordstrom put all its focus on dazzling customers with service beyond what they had ever come to expect.

In many ways Nordstrom is a brilliant example of taking a simple differentiating idea—"better customer service"—and elevating it to a coherent marketing direction. Consider the "company structure," which is an upside down pyramid with you know whom on top:

[Customers]

[Sales and Sales Support People]
▾
[Department Managers]
▾
[Store Managers,
Merchandise Managers,
Buyers]
▾
[Board
of
Directors]

We especially like the employee handbook, which consists of a single five-by-eight card that reads:

WELCOME TO NORDSTROM

We're glad to have you with our Company.
Our number one goal is to provide
outstanding customer service.
Set both your personal and professional goals high.
We have great confidence in your ability to achieve them.

Nordstrom Rules:
Rule #1: Use your good judgment in all situations.
There will be no additional rules.

Please feel free to ask your department manager,
store manager or division general manager
any questions at any time.

How's that for simplicity? Nordstrom is our kind of organization.

In simplest terms the trick is to get new customers and hang onto the ones you've got. The "differentiating idea" is what you use to attract the new ones. But we've written enough about that.

"Hanging onto" is something that companies are now spending more time and money on. New technology has made this possible.

A simple example: I pick up the phone in my hotel room and dial the front desk. A person comes on the line and says: "Good morning, Mr. Trout. What can we do for you?"

That little touch of knowing my name via some communications technology gives me a warm feeling about the service in this hotel. (And at $250 a night, they damn well better know your name.)

If you're interested in learning about how companies are using microchip technology to enhance customer loyalty, you might want to pick up a book entitled *Enterprise One to One* by Don Peppers and Martha Rogers. We would tell you more about it, but it's a little too complex for us. This book has 425 pages and endless ideas about customer service.

But if you want it in simplest terms, the whole "discipline" of customer service is based on two commonsense ideas. You should treat customers so they (1) buy more, and (2) complain less.

Finally, one aspect of a marketing program that is often overlooked is that of reinforcing the perceptions of your existing customers. Make them feel smart about being your customers.

In a program for Ericsson's private radio systems, the differentiating idea was to talk about the "extended life" of an Ericsson system versus a Motorola system. It was an idea based on Ericcson's unique approach to radio spectrum technology.

Obviously, not having a system "become obsolete" was a powerful benefit to a prospect considering a multimillion dollar radio investment. But it also dramatically reinforced Ericsson customers by making their investment look smart.

The most avid readers of automotive advertising are customers who just bought a car. They want reinforcement for their purchase. Then they go out and tell their friends and neighbors about the wonderful car they've bought.

While many CEOs love to talk about customer orientation, it's interesting to see where the most successful actually spend their time. In an Inc. Magazine survey, CEOs of the 500 list of fastest-growing private companies were asked about their greatest concerns. Here is their response:

- Competitive strategies 18%
- Managing people 17%
- Keeping up with technology 13%
- Managing growth 13%
- Managing finances 12%

You'll notice that "customers" didn't even make the list.

A SIMPLE SUMMATION

It's not about knowing your customer. It's about your customer knowing about you.

CHAPTER 9

Annual budgets

A simple way to maximize your dollars

I gave him an unlimited budget and he exceeded it.

— Edward Bennett Williams

When you have a big winner, you want to go for broke. You want to pour it on. Your biggest protection from competitive inroads is a massive investment in resources. If you don't move fast enough, you let your competitors reap the rewards that your efforts have sown.

One problem is the annual budget. While a nice way to keep track of the money, it creates a system that has little flexibility in accommodating change.

Can you imagine a war based on an annual budget? It would go something like this: "Sorry, Colonel, you'll have to wait until January for reinforcements. That's when we get our new budget." The problem here is the missed opportunity.

Your program launch might result in a big mistake by your major competitor. The opportunity to exploit this opening could call for an important increase in money and effort. When next year's budget rolls around, it may be too late.

But it's no matter whether or not we dislike the annual budget, it's here to stay. That being the case, we have spent many years searching for a system that took a fixed amount of money and spent it to maximum advantage. This search took place primarily in the land of big multi-product companies with big budgets. This is where most of the "spending your money more wisely" problems reside.

The money problems of small, single-product companies tend to be more of obtaining enough money to spend. They usually don't have enough money to waste. (So if you're one of these, we suggest that you move on to the next chapter.)

Now, for you that are left, let's analyze how money is usually spent in multiproduct companies. It can usually best be described as a "bits and pieces" system. Every product develops its own budget. Our experience shows that the number that is set is usually based more on sales volume than anything else.

In terms of budgeting, the question that we hear more than any other is, "What percent of sales do companies usually spend on marketing?" *Our answer:* "Enough to do the job."

The problem with this approach is that some products, the ones with smaller sales, suffer from underspending. On the other side of the coin, established products often get the lion's share of the budget, whether it's needed or not. And who is going to admit that it's not needed or it's being wasted?

What this often means is that new products and ideas end up with insufficient funds. Your bigger budget request is usually met by this kind of remark, "Come back with that request when your numbers are better." But how are they to get better without enough money to do the job?

And all products in this system suffer from inflexibility. Once the money is put into different pots, product by product, it's all but impossible to retrieve that money. This kind of fragmentation makes it impossible to suddenly seize new opportunities or take advantage of a competitive situation. It's "Nice idea, Harry. Come back to us next year when there's a new budget."

The problem is that in this high speed world new opportunities don't hang around very long. Someone else seizes the moment.

Those are the traditional problems of your typical budgeting process. Now here's an untraditional approach that maximizes that annual pot of money—one that can get a certain number of jobs done properly.

Step 1. Prepare Marketing Plans. Develop plans that position each product in terms of its marketing life cycle. Is it a new market? How established is the competition? What's the competitive mental angle? Where are you in terms of distribution? What's the awareness or perception of your product and that of the competition?

These plans should be candid and based on hard reality. No wishful thinking.

Step 2. Rank Product Opportunities. This is where the numbers come in as you determine which products offer the most profit potential if the job gets done properly. Can this product or service command a price premium? Is it a new-generation idea that can help you establish leadership? Is it a commodity business with established competition?

This step does require educated guesswork, because you can't predict the future. What you're trying to do is rate each move to determine which one has the best chance to pay off the best.

We'll give you a rating hint: Rate your competition in each battle. The weaker the competition, the better your chance for success. Competing against big well-trained armies isn't much fun.

Step 3. Assign Advertising Tasks. Since advertising tends to be the most expensive part of a marketing plan, it's important to make sure you spend your advertising money where it can do the most good. And spend enough of it to do the job.

For example, advertising is especially useful in creating awareness about new ideas or new products. It can also be very powerful in comparing your product with that of a competitor (dramatizing your competitive mental angle).

Advertising isn't very effective when you're trying to persuade or change the mind of a prospect. (In fact, that's impossible.) Advertising isn't very effective if it's just entertaining your prospects and not driving that "difference" into their minds.

Step 4. Stop When You're Out of Money. This is where a CEO has to be thick-skinned and ruthless.

Once you've prioritized your different programs by profit potential and effective tasks, you start at the top and work down. If all you can afford is three major programs, so be it. When you've reached your total limit, the next programs in line are out of luck. They'll have to wait for next year and get by with a minimum of effort. While there is sure to be some gnashing of teeth, what you're trying to avoid is having a lot of money spread around over too many projects. You want maximum returns for maximum effort.

One final note: This process was described as a company process. In a very large company, you could set up this approach on a divisional basis. In other words, each division head would develop his or her budgets using the same methodology.

What's critical in this approach is the total involvement of top management. This is an allocation game, not a spread-it-around game. You're not spending money against the status quo. You're trying to better allocate your money toward future opportunities. And you're making sure that you spend enough to get each job done.

A SIMPLE SUMMATION

Put your money where your opportunities are, not where they were.

CHAPTER 10

Prices

Simple guidelines to get them right

A thing is worth whatever the buyer will pay for it.

— Pubilius Syrus
A Roman writer, first century B.C.

Old Pubilius was our kind of guy. He understood the essence of pricing and got it down to 11 words. Unfortunately, the academics and consultants moved in during the ensuing centuries and made pricing a little more complex.

If you were to pick up a typical marketing text, you'd probably find pricing described in several very wordy chapters and endless charts dedicated to hopelessly confusing some aspiring business student. We especially like this one that combines the marginal cost and marginal revenue concepts for optimal profit (whatever all that means).

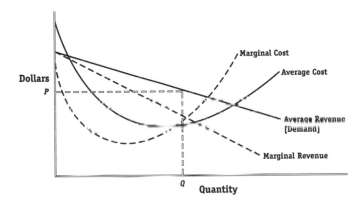

Another interesting piece of nonsense is figuring out what to charge via the "selection of pricing objectives." Take a look.

By the time you've worked your way through this one, we suspect you would find that two or three competitors have already run off with the market.

But then you might say, that's unfair. No one pays attention to textbooks once he or she is out of school.

All right, how about a relatively new book entitled *Power Pricing: How Managing Price Transforms the Bottom Line.*[12] Written by a Harvard professor and a German business consultant, it has 416 pages packed with current pricing concepts and trends. They proudly cover "the mathematical foundations and relationships of price, cost and profit as well as discussions of international, nonlinear, and product pricing and price time customization and bundling." (Boy, that will put you to sleep at night.)

We honestly don't know whether all this theory is nonsense or brilliance buried in complexity. What we do know is that there are some practical pricing considerations that have been proven over and over in the marketplace. Most of them revolve not around complex mathematics but around competition.

You've Got to Stay in the Ballpark. When markets are established, ballpark pricing levels are quickly understood by the market. As our Roman friend said at the beginning of the chapter, what "the buyer will pay" is established. If your product's price is out of the ballpark, so to speak, you run the risk of your customers beginning to question whether they are paying too much. This opens the door for your competitors to take your business. Marlboro realized this on "Marlboro Friday," the day it dropped its prices and thus its stock price but gegan to get its business back.

People Will Pay a Little More for Perceived Value. Just as long as you're in the ballpark, your customers will take the pricier box seats if they feel they are getting their money's worth.

Procter & Gamble, by moving down to everyday low prices, has made life more difficult for the store brands. People will pay a little more for a real brand with real benefits. They just won't pay a lot more.

High-Quality Products Should Be More Expensive. People expect to pay more for a better product, but the quality should be visible in some way. A jar of Orville Redenbacher gourmet popping corn looks a lot more impressive than a less expensive can of Jolly Time. It also promises the benefit of popping almost all of the kernels.

If I'm paying more for a NorthFace outdoor jacket, it's helpful if I have that GoreTex label hanging on it that says "guaranteed to keep you dry." My Rolex should look sturdy and substantial. But, to be honest, a lot of watches at a fraction of the Rolex price look sturdy and substantial. This raises the next point.

High-Priced Products Should Offer Prestige. If I've spent $5000 for a Rolex, I want my friends and neighbors to know I'm wearing a Rolex. It's how they know I'm successful. So it is with expensive cars. While they will never admit it, the reason people spend $50,000 for a car is to impress their friends and neighbors.

Therein lies the reason why the Cadillac Allante was a $50,000 bomb. Would my neighbors be impressed with a "Cadillac"? Where's the prestige? How will my neighbors know I spent $50,000 for an automobile?

What does a high price say about the product? It says the product is worth a lot. In essence, the high price becomes an inherent benefit of the product itself. (This is one of the powerful motivating factors in the success of many high-end flanking moves—Mercedes-Benz automobiles, Absolut vodka, Grey Poupon mustard, to name three examples.)

Late Entrants Usually Enter on Price. When there's a strongly established leader, new competitors usually use low price as a strategy.

What you don't want to do is let them get established. Kodak let Fuji get established by not moving quickly to counter Fuji's prices. AT&T let MCI get almost 20 percent of the market before it moved to blunt MCI's price attack.

Military generals have a saying about dealing with invading troops. "You should stop them in the water where they are weakest. Next, stop them on the beaches where they are still weak and unformed. Never let them get inland."

The classic blocking move of all time not only smashed a competitive move, but also catapulted the brand to the position of the best-selling drugstore product in America.

The brand is Tylenol, an acetaminophen product marketed by Johnson & Johnson's McNeil Laboratories. Originally priced 50 percent higher than aspirin and promoted mainly to physicians and other health care specialists, Tylenol was headed up the sales charts.

The people at Bristol-Meyers thought they saw an opportunity. So in June 1975 Bristol-Meyers introduced Datril with the "same pain reliever, same safety as Tylenol." The difference is the price, said Datril ads, which quoted $2.85 as the price of 100 Tylenol tablets and $1.85 for Datril.

One of the mistakes Bristol-Meyers made was to market-test the idea in its traditional test markets, Albany and Peoria. Any guess who was watching the test with eagle eyes?

Two weeks before the Datril advertising broke, Johnson & Johnson notified Bristol-Meyers that it was cutting Tylenol's price to match Datril's. Furthermore, Johnson & Johnson also issued credit memorandums to reduce prices on existing stocks in stores.

The Johnson & Johnson response worked perfectly. Datril never achieved more than a 1 percent market share.

Tylenol, on the other hand, took off like a rocket. The momentum created by Tylenol's response lifted the brand to the top and to this day there is no perceived no. two in the category. Johnson & Johnson has acetaminophen country all to itself.

High Prices and High Profits Attract Competitors. Like bears to honey, your competitors will smell your success and flock to get a piece of it.

Smart companies don't milk the market. They keep their prices low so as to eventually dominate the market and discourage new competitors. Microsoft is an example of this approach. It will practically give software away in order to maintain its dominance or to squeeze out a competitor.

In addition, research has shown that a deep price cut sooner rather than later can propel a new product's sales.

While it's tempting to maximize your profits in a new category, remember that you're also encouraging a competitor to look at what you're doing and say, "Hey, I can do that for a lot less and still make money."

Don't Train Your Customers to Buy on Price. Some categories tend to self-destruct by always being on sale. Mink coats and mattresses seem never to be sold at anything near a list price. Sometimes, Detroit gets rebate happy and the market just waits for a deal. Lately it's the endless deals on cellular phones.

We're not saying you can ignore price competition. But there are dos and don'ts of discounting. Here's a chart you might want to keep handy for the next time someone wants you to drop your prices.

The commandments of discounting

- Thou shalt not offer discounts because everyone else does.
- Thou should be creative with your discounting.
- Thou should use discounts to clear stocks or generate extra business.
- Thou should put time limits on the deal.
- Thou should make sure the ultimate customer gets the deal.
- Thou should discount only to survive in a mature market.
- Thou should stop discounting as soon as you can.

It's Hard to Win with a Low Price. Positioning yourself with a high price is one thing. Using "low price" as your strategy is another. Few companies find happiness with this approach for the simple reason that all of your competitors have access to a pencil. With it, they can mark down their prices any time they want. And there goes your advantage. As Michael Porter says, "Cutting prices is usually insanity if the competition can go as low as you can."

And marking up prices only works if your competition follows you. In the summer of 1997, General Mills raised prices by an average of 2.6 percent. The other cereal makers stayed pat, and General Mills's core brand sales dropped by 11 percent the next quarter.

Low prices only work where you have a structured, low-cost advantage over your competition. Southwest Airlines has cost advantages over the major airlines (no unions, one kind of airplane, no reservation system, etc.). This has enabled Southwest to successfully position itself as a low-fare airline.

The U.S. Postal Service has positioned its Priority Mail service as a low-cost alternative to UPS and FedEx. Priority Mail doesn't offer fancy electronic tracking systems and next day delivery so the Postal Service can keep its costs down while taking a little extra time to deliver. This approach appears to be working quite well for the U.S. Postal Service though we suspect its competitors are beginning to look at their pencils.

Prices Can Go Down. With capacity growing, currencies tumbling, and competition increasing, the old rules have changed. Prices are headed down. This can call for new strategies such as adding value in unique ways. General Electric does this by advising customers on the nuances of doing business around the globe. GE also added service capability so its customers didn't have to keep service people on staff.

Other companies quickly simplified their product lines by shedding unpopular products. The result is fewer losers and fewer losses in share and profits.

Some find ways to decrease costs faster than pricing falls. They do this by using information technology to buy more from fewer suppliers and thus get the best possible volume pricing.

The trick is to face this kind of reality, get to know it, and make it your friend.

Make Sure You Build Some Promotional Dollars into Your Price. One of the most common mistakes we see in pricing is not allocating an adequate amount of dollars to build your brand. Usually some marketing expense is built in, but it often isn't enough to build the perceived value of the brand.

What also isn't considered is that building a differentiated brand requires some up front money. Sophisticated marketers "investment spend." They take no earnings early in the process—instead they plow sales back into brand building.

How are you going to build perceived value without those dollars to present your differentiating idea to your prospects? And as we've said in an earlier chapter, without that idea you had better have a very low price.

A SIMPLE SUMMATION

A thing is worth whatever the buyer will pay for it and your competition will let you charge.

Leadership Issues

Running a company in this competitive world is like running a war. It has to run with what the military call the KISS principle. (Keep it simple stupid.)

CHAPTER 11

Mission statements

All they add is needless confusion

A bunch of guys take off their ties and coats, go into a motel room for three days, and put a bunch of words on a piece of paper—and then go back to business as usual.

— General Manager John Rock
GM Oldsmobile Division, on
company mission statements

One could assume that once a company understands its basic differentiating strategy, it would be a simple matter to sit down and fold it into a mission statement.

Don't make that assumption.

Since Volvo is all about safety, its mission statement would read something like: "Volvo is in business to make the safest vehicles in the world."

Do you think Volvo has anything like that hanging on its walls? Nope. It has a mission statement of 130 words and "safety" shows up as the 126th word. (It barely made it into the statement.)

It's no wonder that Volvo is drifting into hot, sporty models and convertibles like its C70. On these cars, gone is that safe "tanky" look. If it keeps this up, gone will be its business as well.

Mission statements are a relatively new phenomenon in business. Pamela Goett, the editorial director of the *Journal of Business Strategy*, put their beginnings as follows:

> "A handful of years ago, some guru opined that mission statements were absolutely critical to a company's success. So a lot of firms packed their most senior people off to expensive retreats to prepare this vital document. And the executives took the task very, very seriously (which is why so many mission statements sound so stuffy). The hoopla over mission statements and vision has a lot in common with the cheers for the emperor's new clothes. It's applause for delusions, for quick fixes for something that needs more thought and planning than can be expressed in a calligraphic paragraph.[13]"

It's current thinking that a mission statement helps define what a company wants to be when it grows up. Companies spend weeks and months agonizing over every word.

If you explore this thinking, you'll see there is a widely accepted process for creating these statements. The following chart presents the phases of effort along with our remarks about the problems that we see with each phase.

How mission statements are born

Phase 1: Envision the future.

(It can't be done.)

Phase 2: Form a mission task force.

(Waste the time of expensive people.)

Phase 3: Develop a draft statement.

(Many hands make things mushy.)

Phase 4: Communicate the final statement.

(Hang it on the wall for people to ignore.)

Phase 5: Operationalize the statement.

(Turn the company into mush.)

As far as we are concerned this process adds needless complication to most companies and very little benefit.

Nothing proves this point more than glancing through a book called *The Mission Statement Book*,[14] which contains 301 corporate mission statements from America's top companies. In an article in *Marketing Magazine*,[15] a gentleman named Jeremy Bullmore sat down and counted the words most frequently used by mission statement writers. It was an exercise in counting the clichés. Here's his tally from the 301 statements:

service (230 times)	growth (118)
customers (211)	environment (117)
quality (194)	profit (114)
value (183)	leader (104)
employees (157)	best (102)

He also discovered that many of these 301 statements are interchangeable. (Could it be that companies are knocking off other companies' mission statements?)

Just for fun, we jotted down a few in the Bs (and a few others). Boise Cascade wrote: "To continuously improve the company's long-term value to customers, employees, shareholders, and society." (Now that could be any company, any time, any place.)

Ben & Jerry, the ice cream people, were a lot more wordy:

> "We are dedicated to the creation and demonstration of a new corporate concept of linked prosperity: Our mission consists of three inter-related parts:
>
> Product Mission: To make, distribute, and sell the finest quality, all-natural ice cream and related products in a wide variety of innovative flavors made from Vermont dairy products.
>
> Underlying the mission of Ben & Jerry's is the determination to hold a deep respect for individuals, inside and outside the company, and for the communities of which they are a part."

(We're all for respecting individuals, but Ben & Jerry need more respect for Haagen Dazs if they are to succeed.)

Boeing wrote about "a fundamental goal of achieving 20 percent average annual return on stockholder's equity." (That's not realistic when you consider Airbus and the struggling Asian economies. Boeing should be talking about the business, not the numbers.)

Even the government is into the act. The Air Force had one of the best of the bunch. "To defend the United States through control and exploitation of air and space." (Kicking ass in the air is indeed what it's about.)

The CIA had almost 200 words of motherhood and mush and not one mention about its basic problem of getting it right.

As best we can see, most of these mission statements have little positive impact on a company's business. Levitz Furniture had a mission of "satisfying the needs and expectations of our customers with quality products and services." (That wonderful mission didn't keep it out of bankruptcy.)

Fortunately, most companies put their mission statements in gold frames and hang them in their lobbies where top managers who have their own agendas ignore them.

A simple approach is to forget about "what you want to be." Management should focus its efforts on "what you can be." It's far more productive.

This means that you have to put your basic business strategy into the statement. It should present your differentiating idea and explain how by preempting this idea you will be in a position to outflank your competition. Volvo's mission statement should be about safety. That's what it can continue to represent in the market.

Boeing's mission statement should be about maintaining leadership in the commercial aircraft industry, not about return on equity.

Ben & Jerry's statement should be about making Vermont dairy products the gold standard over the likes of New Jersey's products (New Jersey is where Haagen Dazs is located.)

And you don't need a committee to spend weeks writing this statement. This should be something that the CEO and his or her top people should be able to put together in a morning's work. Keep it short and simple.

The Seagram Company mission statement spills over to 10 sentences and 198 words. (You need a tumbler of good Scotch to get through it.)

After all, if a CEO needs a committee to figure out what the basic business is about, then that company needs a new CEO, not a mission statement.

The last step is not to just hang the "what we can do" statement on the wall. Take this basic business strategy to all the important groups in a company and make sure they understand it. Let them ask questions. Be candid with your answers.

And to us, that's the only purpose of a mission statement: to make sure everyone in the company gets it.

A SIMPLE SUMMATION

A mushy mission statement is an indication that a company doesn't know where it's going.

CHAPTER 12

Leadership

It's about leading the charge

To lead the people, walk behind them.

— Lao-tzu,
Chinese philosopher and
founder of Taoism

Strategy, vision, and mission statements are dependent on the simple premise that you must know where you're going. No one can follow you if you don't know where you're headed.

Many years ago, in a book called *The Peter Principle*, authors Peter and Hull made this observation: "Most hierarchies are nowadays so cumbered with rules and traditions, and so bound in by public laws, that even high employees do not have to lead anyone anywhere, in the sense of pointing out the direction and setting the pace. They simply follow precedents, obey regulations, and move at the head of the crowd. Such employees lead only in the sense that the carved wooden figure-head leads the ship."

Perhaps this pessimistic view of leadership skills has led to the explosion of hundreds of books dealing with leadership (most of them being downright silly). There's advice on whom to emulate (Atilla the Hun), what to achieve (inner peace), what to study (failure), what to strive for (charisma), whether to delegate (sometimes), whether to collaborate (maybe), America's secret leaders (women), the personal qualities of leadership (having integrity), how to achieve credibility (be credible), how to be an authentic leader (find the leader within), the nine natural laws of leadership (don't even ask). In fact, there are 3098 books in print with the word "leader" in the title.

To us, how to be an effective leader isn't worth a whole book. Drucker gets it into a few sentences. "The foundation of effective leadership is thinking through the organization's mission, defining it and establishing it, clearly and visibly. The leader sets the goals, sets the priorities, and sets and maintains the standards."

First, how do you find the proper direction? To become a great strategist, you have to put your mind in the mud of the marketplace. You have to find your inspiration down at the front, in the ebb and flow of the great marketing battles taking place in the mind of the prospect.

It's no secret that most of the world's greatest military strategists started at the bottom. And they maintained their edge by never losing touch with the realities of war. Karl von Clausewitz did not attend the best military schools, did not serve in the field under the best military minds, and did not learn his profession from his superiors. Clausewitz learned his military strategy the best way and the hardest way—by serving in the front line at some of the bloodiest and most famous battles of military history.

The unpretentious Sam Walton traveled to the front lines of every one of his Wal-Mart stores throughout his life. He even spent time in the middle of the night on the loading docks, talking with the crews.

Unlike "Mister Sam," many chief executives tend to lose touch. The bigger the company, the more likely it is that the chief executive has lost touch with the front lines. This might be the single most important factor limiting the growth of a corporation.

All other factors favor size. Marketing is war, and the first principle of warfare is the principle of force. The larger army, the larger company, has the advantage. But the larger company gives up some of that advantage if it cannot keep itself focused on the marketing battle that takes place in the mind of the customer.

The shootout at General Motors between Roger Smith and Ross Perot illustrates the point. When he was on the GM board, Ross Perot spent his weekends buying cars. He was critical of Roger Smith for not doing the same.

"We've got to nuke the GM system," Perot said. He advocated atom-bombing the heated garages, chauffeur-driven limousines, and executive dining rooms.

Chauffeur-driven limousines for a company trying to sell cars? Top management's disconnection with the marketplace is the biggest problem facing big business.

If you're a busy CEO, how do you gather objective information on what is really happening? How do you get around the propensity of middle management to tell you what they think you want to hear? How do you get the bad news as well as the good?

If you don't get the bad news directly, bad ideas can flourish instead of being killed. Consider the following parable:

THE PLAN
In the beginning was the Plan.
And then came the Assumptions.
And the Assumptions were without form.
And the Plan was completely without substance.

THE WORKERS
And the darkness was upon the face of the workers
as they spake unto their Group Head saying:
"It is a crock of shit and it stinketh."

THE GROUP HEADS
And the Group Heads went unto their Section Heads and sayeth:
"It is a pail of dung and none may abide by the odor thereof."

THE SECTION HEADS
And the Section Heads went unto their Managers and sayeth unto them:
"It is a container of excrement. And it is very strong.
Such that none may abide by it."

THE MANAGERS
And the Managers went unto their Director and sayeth unto him:
"It is a vessel of fertilizer. And none may abide by its strength."

THE DIRECTOR
And the Director went into the Vice President and sayeth unto him:
"It promoteth growth and is very powerful."

THE VICE PRESIDENT
And the VP went unto the President and sayeth unto him:
"This powerful new Plan will actively promote the growth
and efficiency of the Company."

THE POLICY
And the President looked upon the Plan and saw
that it was good and the Plan became Policy.

One possibility of finding out what's really going on is "going in disguise" or poking around unannounced. This would be especially useful at the distributor or retailer level. In many ways this is analogous to the king who dresses up as a commoner and mingles with his subjects. *The reason*: To get honest opinions of what's happening.

Like kings, chief executives rarely get honest opinions from their ministers. There's just too much intrigue going on at the court.

The members of the sales force, if you have one, are a critical element in the equation. The trick is how to get a good, honest evaluation of the competition out of them. The best thing you can do is to praise honest information. Once the word gets around that a CEO prizes honesty and reality, a lot of good information will be forthcoming.

Another aspect of the problem is the allocation of your time. Quite often it is taken up with too many activities that keep you from visiting the front. Too many boards, too many committees, too many testimonial dinners. According to one survey, the average CEO spends 30 percent of his or her time on "outside activities." He or she spends 17 hours a week preparing for meetings.

Since the typical top executive works 61 hours a week, that leaves only 20 hours for everything else, including managing the operation and going down to the front.

No wonder chief executives delegate the marketing function. But that's a mistake.

Marketing is too important to be turned over to an underling. If you delegate anything, you should delegate the chairmanship of the next fund-raising drive. (As you've perhaps noticed, the vice president of the United States attends the state funerals, not the president.)

The next thing to cut back on is meetings. Instead of talking things over, go out and see for yourself. As General Secretary Gorbachev told President Reagan, on the occasion of the president's first trip to the Soviet Union, "It is better to see once than to hear a hundred times."

You have to put your mind on the tactics of the battle you want to win. You have to focus on your competitors and their strengths and weaknesses in the mind. You have to search out that one attribute or differentiating idea that will work in the mental battleground.

Then you have to be willing to focus all your efforts to develop a coherent strategy to exploit that idea.

You also have to be willing to make changes inside the organization in order to exploit the opportunities on the outside.

And you must be a doer. The way to quickly spot a nonleader is to watch for "should." When a viable suggestion is presented, the would-be leader says, "We should do that." Usually, you discover, those "shoulds" pile up and little gets done.

The real leader never uses the word "should." His or her response to a good suggestion is "Let's do it." Then it's on to the next decision.

The best leaders share their wisdom with the next generation. Noel Tichy, professor at the University of Michigan Business School, says, "Great leaders have to be great teachers." He estimates that Jack Welch, GE's revered chairman and CEO, devotes 30 percent of his time to leadership development. (Welch even teaches once a week at GE's executive training institute.) "That's where he gets his leverage," claims Professor Tichy.

CEO Andy Grove personally teaches Intel Corp.'s orientation program for managers. When PepsiCo CEO Roger Enrico was vice chairman, he spent 110 days over an 18-month span coaching high-potential executives.

The best leaders know that direction alone is no longer enough. The best leaders are storytellers, cheerleaders, and facilitators. They reinforce their sense of direction or vision with words and action.

There is no greater leader in the airline business than Herb Kelleher, the chairman of Southwest Airlines. He has become the king of the low-fare, short-haul airline business. Year after year, his airline is on every list of the "most admired" and "most profitable" companies.

If you've flown Southwest, you've probably recognized the incredible spirit and enthusiasm of the airline personnel. They even have a sense of humor that, as one passenger put it, "makes flying on that cattle car enjoyable."

Anybody that knows Herb realizes that the airline's personality is Herb's personality. He is an amazing cheerleader who keeps those planes moving and morale high. He is indeed "walking behind them."

He also knows his people and his business. In a meeting with Herb, we were encouraging him to buy one of the East Coast shuttles that were for sale. It would instantly make Southwest a big player in the East.

He thought a minute and said, "I sure would like their gates in New York, Washington and Boston. But what I don't want is their airplanes and, more importantly, their people."

He sure was right. Cheerleading those East Coast shuttle people would have been impossible.

Herb Kelleher points to another attribute of your best leaders. They tend to live the business and come to personify it. In the heyday of Chase Manhattan Bank, its chairman, David Rockefeller, created news just by visiting foreign heads of state. In effect, he was a head of state.

In his prime, Lee Iacocca personified Chrysler.

Today, Bill Gates personifies Microsoft. He looks like a computer nerd. He sounds like a computer nerd. He lives in a computer nerd's house.

While everyone knows Mr. Gates, very few know Dino Cortopassi. He is the king of "real Italian tomato sauce" that he supplies to the 60,000 or so real Italian pizzerias and restaurants in America—the red sauce places.

Dino has come to personify "real Italian," which is his differentiating idea. He lives in an Italian villa. He makes sausage. He has vineyards. He has his own boccie court. Every year he goes to Italy to visit his relatives. He sends his important customers the family's olive oil. Just as Mr. Gates dominates the software world, Dino dominates the market for fresh-packed tomatoes and sauce.

A visible leader is a very powerful weapon with customers and prospects. This kind of leader offers unique credentials for a company. (The Germans had a deep respect for George Patton—so much so that the Allies used him as a decoy.)

Also, the troops are proud to follow this kind of leader into battle. They trust him instinctively. Without trust, there won't be any followers. And without followers you won't have much of a charge.

A SIMPLE SUMMATION

Good leaders know where they are going.

CHAPTER 13

Long-term planning

It's just wishful thinking

Anyone who says businessmen deal in facts, not fiction, has never read old five-year projections.

— Malcolm Forbes

A long-term strategic plan is useless unless you are doing your competitor's plans as well. Yet many CEOs think that complex long-term planning is critical if a company is going to fulfill its mission statement.

If Shakespeare came back as a CEO, he'd be tempted to kill his company's long-term planners as well as its lawyers. And he'd have ample ammunition. Long-term planning didn't make Xerox a factor in office automation. Long-term planning didn't keep GM from losing 15 points of the automotive market in the past 20 years.

It all really began in the early 1960s when General Electric emerged as the pioneer in strategic planning. GE created a large, centralized staff of planners to ponder the future. Consultant McKinsey & Co. helped GE view its products in terms of strategic business units, identify competitors for each, and evaluate its position against them.

But long-term planning really picked up steam in 1963. Under founder Bruce D. Henderson, Boston Consulting Group became the first of many strategy boutiques. BCG pioneered a series of concepts that took corporate America by storm, including the "experience curve" and the "growth and market-share matrix."

Today's enlightened discussion of long-term strategy would include talk about "strategic intent," "white-space opportunities," and "coevolution."

For those of you who've missed the concept of "co-evolving," it talks about "business ecosystems" where companies work cooperatively and competitively to create the next round of innovation. (This sounds like la-la land to us.)

It all comes out of a book entitled *The Death of Competition*. Our question: If competition died, who are those folks trying to take away your business?

Beyond all the nonsense, the fatal flaw in all of this long-term planning is the simple fact that you can't predict the future. History is filled with bold forecasts that didn't pan out. Here's a sampling of predictions that flopped:

- "Airplanes are interesting but of no military value." Marshal Ferdinand Foch, French military strategist, 1911.

- "The horse is here to stay, but the automobile is only a novelty, a fad." President of Michigan Savings Bank, 1903, advising Henry Ford's lawyer not to invest in the Ford Motor Co.

- "What use could this company make of an electrical toy?" Western Union president William Orton, rejecting Alexander Graham Bell's offer to sell his struggling telephone company to Western Union for $100,000.

- "Who the hell wants to hear actors talk?" Harry Warner, Warner Brothers, 1927.

- "We don't like their sound. Groups of guitars are on the way out." Decca Records' statement on rejecting the Beatles, 1962.

- "There is no reason for any individual to have a computer in their home." Kenneth Olsen, founder and president of Digital Equipment Corp., 1977.

Spotting trends is the best you can do about the future. America's health orientation is certainly a trend of which many products have taken advantage.

Also America's shortage of time has become another trend, as working couples seem to have less and less time to even fit in a trip to the dry cleaners. That has given birth to businesses like "commuter cleaners" that pick up and deliver cleaning right to the train station. (Nice idea.)

But trend spotting can be tricky. The most common flaw is extrapolating a trend. According to the red meat predictions of recent years, everyone today would be eating broiled fish or mesquite barbecued chicken. But red meat consumption has gone up (along with cigar smoking). Basic habits change very slowly, and the press often magnifies small changes.

Equally as bad as extrapolating a trend is the common practice of assuming the future will be a replay of the past. When you assume that nothing will change, you are predicting the future just as surely as when you assume that something will change. Remember, the unexpected always happens.

"Futurism" is becoming an industry of its own. Futurists are busy cashing in on tomorrow.

It all began with people like H. G. Wells, Jules Verne, and George Orwell, who were practicing futurists under the guise of science fiction authors. But now it's turned deadly serious. Alvin Toffler (of *Future Shock* fame) even has plans for a nightly TV show called *Next News Now*. Says Mr. Toffler, "There's a History Channel but no Future Channel. We plan to remedy that."

Is this stuff visionary or just plain old forecasting? Paul Saffo of the Institute for the Future has this grand answer: "My job is to help our clients expand their perceived range of possibilities."

Even some futurists are getting uncomfortable with the profession of prognostication. "Futurism isn't prediction anymore," says Douglas Rushkoff, author of the pop-culture chronicle *Cyberia*. "It's state-of-the-art propaganda. It's future creation. Futurists put their clients in a state of fear and then explain that they hold the secret knowledge that can save them."

A variation on the difficulty of predicting the future is trying to research the future.

Not that many years ago, fax machines were found only in a few large offices. Today they are ubiquitous and are rapidly spilling out of the office and into the home. The fax machine is American in invention, technology, design, and development. And U.S. manufacturers had fax machines all ready to be sold. Yet not one fax machine offered for sale in the United State today is American-made.

The Americans did not put the fax machines on the market, because market research convinced them that there was no demand for such a gadget. Despite the well-known fact that one cannot conduct market research on something not in the market, researchers went out and asked people: "Would you buy a telephone accessory that costs upwards of $1500 and enables you to send, for $1 a page, the same letter the post office delivers for 25 cents?" The answer, predictably, came back "no."

What makes more sense in planning is to build some simplicity into the process. Here's what we consider is a better and simpler approach to planning.

> 1. Inform your staff people that predicting the future is an exercise in delusion and that excruciatingly detailed "strategic scenarios" are a waste of time.
>
> 2. Inform everybody that the real value of strategic planning is to give your businesses direction and the means to make progress over competition.
>
> 3. Tell your planning people to sit down with operating executives in each business and discuss those directional guidelines under different economic assumptions.
>
> 4. Emphasize that what you're looking for is a "flight plan" to guide the company—something that will be simpler and less fancy than an old-style formal plan.

In the land of the smaller companies, all this doesn't appear to be too much of a problem. They just don't have an army of planners running around creating 2-pound planning books.

The *Wall Street Journal*[16] reported on Bill Long, the CEO of Waremont Foods, which operates 25 grocery stores from Salem, Oregon, to Idaho Falls. Since Long led an employee takeover in 1985, Waremont's net worth has risen by 1500 percent to $215 million.

Ask Bill Long his plans for the next five years and brace yourself for a tirade. "How the hell should I know?" he bellows. "Tell me where my customers are going to be in five years. My competitors, my capital, my suppliers!"

Ask to see his strategic plan and the reaction's no different. "Written strategies are crazy!" he says. "Instead of strategies you need instant decision making."

He's our kind of guy.

You might wonder what's happening these days at General Electric, the folks who started it all. It might shock you to know that GE is out of long-term planning. Jack Welch nuked GE's central planning department and pushed the responsibility for strategy down to the 12 operating units. They meet with top management over a four-day period. The focus is on strategy both near term and a four-year look into the future. They look at new products and what the competition is doing. No more reports bound in vinyl.

Jack Welch is also our kind of guy.

A SIMPLE SUMMATION

Wishful thinking belongs in fairy-tale land. What you must deal with is reality.

CHAPTER 14

Organization

The simpler, the better

We have met the enemy and he is us.

— Pogo

A good organization drives the correct strategic behavior. Unfortunately, large organizations often become so complex that one part is undoing what another part is doing.

In working for a large telecommunications company, we discovered that it had developed a way to work around any disruption in its network. This very expensive "self-restoring" system would reroute calls around the break in a matter of minutes. We pushed that as company's very powerful differentiating idea only to discover that a part of the company had sold this technology to its competitors.

It's not good enough to have the best strategy or the best financial system or for any single part of an organization to be world class unless all parts are working together in a meaningful way.

To us, the best and simplest analogy comes from Peter Drucker when he compared an organization to a large symphony orchestra. But he warned that it cannot be organized in typical big-business fashion. That would result in a chief conductor, several vicechairmen conductors, and countless vice president conductors.

There must be one conductor to whom every specialist instrumentalist plays directly, because everyone has the same score. In other words, there are no intermediaries between the specialists and the top manager. They are organized as a gigantic task force. The organization is totally flat. What's nice about this approach is that it begins to do away with the rigid, hierarchal organization chart.

In a brilliant 1970 book entitled *Up the Organization*, Robert Townsend had some similar thoughts about effective organization. All he lacked were the musical instruments. He noted: "Good organizations are living bodies that grow new muscles to meet challenges. A chart demoralizes people. Nobody thinks of himself as below other people. And in a good company he isn't. Yet on paper there it is. If you have to circulate something, use a loose-leaf table of organization (like a magazine masthead) instead of a diagram with the people in little boxes. Use alphabetical order by name and by function wherever possible."

But the trick to a good organization is that everyone has to be focused on the same sheet of music.

The reason that conglomerates never worked very well was because you had too many orchestras playing the same hall. And they were playing different kinds of music to boot.

In today's new mergers, conglomerates are out; being number one is in.

This was why Westinghouse sold off its power generation and defense lines of business and expanded into broadcasting. Westinghouse Electric Corp. is now CBS Corp. Michael Jordan, the CEO and conductor of this new orchestra, can now focus on television and radio, where the corporation has a dominant position.

While Westinghouse was a grand old American name, no amount of nostalgia can minimize the harsh reality of excess capacity now haunting many capital-intensive industries, ranging from steel to chemicals, oil refining, auto manufacturing, semiconductors, and parts of retailing. If that overcapacity keeps growing in the next year or so, as some observers predict, the upshot could be even-greater waves of price cutting, sinking profits, and the passing of weak outfits into stronger hands.

Many executives being forced to decide whether to buy or sell—or both—are clearly hesitating to make such decisions and to focus on one line of business. But Mr. Jordan isn't.

In this competitive global economy it's too difficult to try to play too many different kinds of music. Many companies are opting out of their complex organizations and returning to a simpler tune that they know they can play well.

- Eastman Kodak sold its Sterling Winthrop drug unit and two other businesses to focus on its core film operation.

- Sears spun off Allstate, Dean Witter, and Caldwell Banker to focus on retailing.

- Merck has dropped just about all of its nondrug business.

- Guinness PLC divested itself of virtually everything but beer and liquor.

- Union Carbide sold all its noncore assets and eliminated 90 percent of its workforce.

There are two ways to organize your orchestras.

Large companies can field different orchestras playing their music to specialized audiences. This is a multibrand strategy that accommodates changing markets. Hallmark is the number one player in "greeting cards." It has the classic Hallmark line, the Ambassador line for discounters, the Pet Love line for pet owners, and the Shoebox line for humorous cards. That all adds up to almost half the market.

The Vendome Luxury Group has fielded different orchestras playing "luxury." The company's brands include Cartier jewelry, Alfred Dunhill men's products, Montblanc pens, Piaget and Baume & Mercier watches, and others.

Smaller companies in a category have one, specialized orchestra. Volvo plays "safety." Snap-on plays "tools" within its large walk-in vans. H&R Block plays "tax returns." Sun plays UNIX driven "workstations and servers."

Playing one kind of music is not only simpler; it can generate some big numbers.

- Wrigley's plays "gum" to the tune of 37 percent return on equity.

- Intel plays "chips" to the tune of a 20 percent growth rate for the past decade.

- CompUSA plays "retail computers" to the tune of $3 billion in sales.

- Callaway by playing "oversize golf clubs" has become the largest U.S. manufacturer.

This kind of concentration is dictated also by the fact that most of us find it hard enough to do even one thing at a time well, let alone two. Human beings are indeed capable of doing an amazingly wide diversity of things; humanity is a "multipurpose tool." But the way to apply that great range productively is to bring to bear a large number of individual capabilities on one task. It is concentration in which all faculties are focused on one achievement.

We rightly consider keeping many balls in the air a circus stunt. Yet even the juggler does it only for 10 minutes or so. If he were to try doing it longer, he would soon drop all the balls.

Can you imagine all the balls in the air over at the planned merger of Citicorp and Travelers? To us it sounds like the mother of all complex organizations.

Finally, some words about decentralization. Continuing the orchestra analogy, this is where a company gives control of different parts of the orchestra to different conductors.

Conventional wisdom says that decentralization is good. It gets you closer to the market. Our view is that decentralization is bad. It dissipates your forces, adds to complication, and makes it difficult to keep things focused.

Just being closer to the market is no advantage if you are not organized to make a bold move. Take ITT, which had become an unmanageable, complex mess. Most of the businesses acquired by Harold Geneen are now being sold off, but the real problem is ITT's core business, telecommunications. At this stage of the game, ITT should have been in the same league as IBM and AT&T.

To add insult to injury, ITT threw in the towel on its telecommunications business, the jewel of the ITT crown. Compagnie General d'Electricite, a state-owned French conglomerate, now owns ITT Telecommunications.

My ex-partner, Al Ries, in his book *Focus*, puts decentralization in a clear focus.

"If nothing ever changed, a decentralized company would be more efficient and effective than a centralized company. There's no question that decentralization contributes to a sense of responsibility on the part of both the operating unit's management and employees. But how does a decentralized company develop a focus? It doesn't. Decentralization removes top management's ability to point the company in one specific direction. And then to change that direction when conditions in the marketplace change. Decentralization is efficient, but inflexible."

It's better to run an inefficient but centralized company with a powerful market-oriented focus, one that can introduce new music when it's needed. Employees would rather work for a winner than a loser; no matter how much motivation the loser's management provides.

Digital Equipment was a company that fell victim to decentralization's allure. Under a massive restructuring plan, the company reorganized into semiautonomous business units that were able to set their own advertising, pricing, and marketing strategies. While Digital decentralized, it watched its lead in 64-bit workstations disappear. Now the company is in the process of disappearing, as Compaq owns it.

Almost by definition, a decentralized company cannot have a focus on a correct strategic behavior or strategy. It can only serve as a center for accumulating financial results and disseminating them to investors and analysts. What the decentralized company misses the most is the opportunity to jump on and dominate the next-generation concept and use its force.

3M is everybody's favorite decentralized company. While the company continues to churn out a host of "coatings" products (66,000 at last count), there seems to be a shortage of revolutionary new products that could carry the company to new levels of success. The last big winner was Post-it notes, a product introduced in 1980.

Sales at Minnesota Mining and Manufacturing are up 33 percent since 1988, but profits have been relatively flat. 3M could easily miss a big idea hidden in its laboratories with all that decentralization.

The company is just too complicated. There are just too many people running around in too many directions. There is no clear strategic direction or focus.

There's no music, just sounds.

A SIMPLE SUMMATION

The future belongs to a well-organized and well-focused company.

CHAPTER 15

Marketing

It's turning simple ideas into strategy

Marketing, in the fullest sense, is the name of the game. So it better be handled by the boss and his line. Not staff hecklers.

— Robert Townsend
Up the Organization

If a CEO conducts the symphony, it's marketing that oversees the arrangement of the music.

Academics have written tomes about the complexity of marketing and all its functions. Ad agencies and consultants have constructed convoluted systems for building brands. One of our favorite pieces of complexity comes from a U.K. consulting firm that claims a brand has nine positioning elements in a customer's mind: functional needs, objective effects, functional roles, attributes, core evaluators, psychological drives, psychological roles, subjective character, and psychological needs. Then the consultants turn all this into a "bridge matrix."

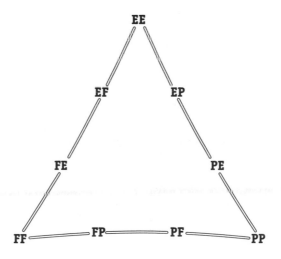

(Help, I'm trapped on a bridge to nowhere.)

Another piece of complexity is the following that some agency is pushing.

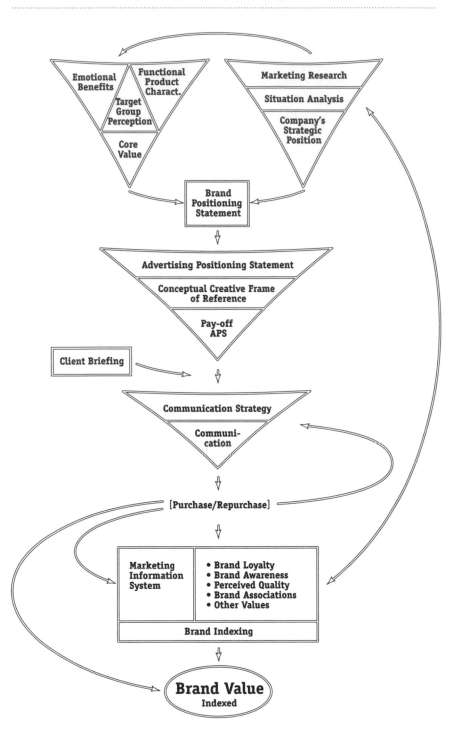

(Help, I'm trapped in a marketing labyrinth.)

We'll give you the essence of marketing in two sentences: First, it's marketing's responsibility to see that everyone is playing the same tune in unison. Second, it's marketing's assignment to turn that tune or differentiating idea into what we call a coherent marketing direction.

The notion of a differentiating idea requires some thought. What kind of idea? Where do you find one? These are the initial questions that must be answered.

In order to help you answer these questions, we propose using the following specific definition. A differentiating idea is a *competitive mental angle.*

This kind of idea must have a *competitive* angle in order to have a chance for success. This does not necessarily mean a better product or service, but rather there must be an element of differentness. It could be smaller, bigger, lighter, heavier, cheaper, or more expensive. It could be a different distribution system.

Furthermore, the idea must be competitive in the total marketing arena, not just competitive in relation to one or two other products or services. For example, Volkswagen's decision in the late fifties to introduce the "first" small car was an excellent competitive idea. At the time General Motors was manufacturing nothing but big, heavily chromed patrol boats. The Beetle was a runaway success.

The VW Beetle was not the first small car on the market, of course. But it was the first car to occupy the "small" position in the mind. It made a virtue out of its size, while the others apologized for their small size by talking about "roominess."

"Think small," said the Volkswagen ads.

An example of a new bad idea is Volvo's sporty coupe and convertible. We see no competitive angle against BMW, Mercedes, and Audi (just to name a few).

Second, a differentiating idea must have a competitive *mental* angle. In other words, the battle takes place in the mind of the prospect.

Competitors that do not exist in the mind can be ignored. There were plenty of pizza places with home delivery operations when John Schnatter launched Papa John's. But nobody owned the "better ingredients" position in the mind.

On the other hand, there are competitors who enjoy strong perceptions that do not agree with reality. It's the perception that must be considered in the selection of an idea, not the reality.

A competitive mental *angle* is the point in the mind that allows your marketing program to work effectively. That's the point you must leverage to achieve results.

But an idea is not enough. To complete the process, you need to turn the idea into a strategy. (If the idea is a nail, the strategy is the hammer.) You need both to establish a position in the mind.

What's a strategy? A strategy is not a goal. Like life itself, a strategy ought to focus on the journey, not the goal. Top-down thinkers are goal-oriented. They first determine what it is they want to achieve, and then they try to devise ways and means to achieve their goals. (More on this in Chapter 17.)

But most goals are simply not achievable. Goal setting tends to be an exercise in frustration. Marketing, like politics, is the art of the possible.

When Roger Smith took over General Motors in 1981, he predicted that GM would eventually own 70 percent of the traditional Big Three domestic car market, up from about 66 percent in 1979. To prepare for this awesome responsibility, GM began a $50 billion modernization program. Boy, was Roger wrong.

Currently, General Motors' share of the Big Three domestic market is 30 percent and falling. His goal was simply not achievable because it was not based on a sound idea.

In our definition, a strategy is not a goal. It's a *coherent marketing direction*. A strategy is *coherent* in the sense that it is focused on the idea that has been selected. Volkswagen had a big tactical success with the small car, but it failed to elevate this idea to a coherent strategy. It forgot about "small" and instead elected to bring into the U.S. market a family of big, fast, and expensive Volkswagens. But other car manufacturers had already preempted these automotive ideas. This opened the way for the Japanese to take over the small car idea.

Second, a strategy encompasses coherent *marketing* activities. Product, pricing distribution, advertising—all the activities that make up the marketing mix must be coherently focused on the idea. (Think of a differentiating idea as a particular wavelength of light and the strategy as a laser tuned to that wavelength. You need both to penetrate the mind of the prospect.)

Finally, a strategy is a coherent marketing *direction*. Once the strategy is established, the direction shouldn't be changed.

The purpose of the strategy is to mobilize your resources to preempt the differentiating idea. By committing all your resources to one strategic direction you maximize the exploitation of the idea without the limitation that the existence of a goal implies.

What are you looking for? You are looking for an angle—a fact, an idea, a concept, an opinion on the part of the prospect that conflicts with the positions held by your competitors.

Take laundry detergents, for example. What does detergent advertising suggest that customers are looking for? Cleanliness. That's why Tide gets clothes "white." Cheer gets clothes "whiter than white." And Bold goes all the way to "bright."

Did you ever watch a person take clothes out of a dryer? If you read the ads, you might think he or she puts on sunglasses so the glare won't ruin the eyes.

In fact, most people hardly look at the clothes at all. But they almost always smell them to see if they smell "fresh." This observation led Unilever to introduce Surf, a detergent whose sole distinguishing characteristic is that it contains twice as much perfume as the competition. *Result:* Surf came in and grabbed a respectable piece of the $3.5 billion U.S. detergent market.

Did you ever watch a commuter buy a cup of coffee to carry on a train or bus? The commuter will often carefully rip a drinking hole in the lid so the coffee won't spill while he or she is drinking it during the trip.

Someone at the Handi-Kup Division of Dixie Products noticed. Handi-Kup introduced a plastic lid with the drinking hole built in.

Some angles are hard to spot because customers express them in the negative. The Adolph Coors Company invented light beer. (Even today there are fewer calories in regular Coors than in Michelob Light.) Yet Coors ignored its own invention until Miller introduced Lite beer.

It was hard to ignore. Before Lite saw the light of day, any Denver bartender could have told you how their customers ordered a Coors. "Give me a Colorado Kool-Aid."

Coors could have preempted the light category with a major advertising program. It didn't. Miller did. So Miller Lite became the first successful light beer.

Most angles are hard to spot because they almost never look like big winners in advance. (If they did, others would already be using them.) Marketing bombshells burst very quickly.

"Great ideas," said Albert Camus, "come into the world as gently as doves. Perhaps then, if we listen attentively, we shall hear amid the uproar of empires and nations a faint flutter of wings, the gentle stirring of life and hope." (See Chapter 16 for advice on how to listen for new ideas.)

When you saw your first bottle of Lite beer, did you say, "This brand is going to become one of the biggest-selling beers in America"? Or did you say, "Here's another Gablinger's"? (The first low calorie beer.)

When you saw the first Toys "Я" Us store, did you say, "This is going to be a $10 billion business selling one-fourth of all the toys in America"? Or did you say to yourself, "Why did they make the letter R backward?"

Did you buy a McDonald's franchise in 1955 when it would have cost you all of $950? Or did you wait in line saying to yourself, "How can they make money selling hamburgers for 15 cents?"

Did you buy Xerox stock in 1958? Andy Warhol soup cans in 1968? A condo in Manhattan in 1979?

Did you save your baseball cards? Your Superman comic books?

Opportunities are hard to spot because they don't look like opportunities. They look like angles—a lighter beer, a more expensive car, a cheaper hamburger, a store that sells only toys. Marketing's responsibility is to take that angle or idea and build it into a strategy so as to unleash its power.

Market leader Pizza Hut could have neutralized one or two Papa John's "better ingredients" delivery units. With the strategy of expanding into a nationwide chain of better ingredient delivery units, Papa John's effectively drove a powerful wedge into the competition. It is first into the mind with this idea.

The idea dictates the strategy. Then the strategy drives the idea. To say that one is more important than the other is to miss the essence of the process. It's the relationship between the two that is the crucial aspect of marketing success.

What's more important in aircraft design: the engine or the wing? Neither. It's the relationship between the two that determines whether your design will get off the runway.

The idea differentiates your business from your competitor's. Strategy gives wing to the idea that can make your business soar.

A SIMPLE SUMMATION

Show me the idea.

CHAPTER 16

New ideas

Something borrowed is simpler

Your idea needs to be original only in its adaptation to the problem you are currently working on.

— Thomas Edison

There are companies that try to turn ideation into a gimmicky science.

In an old mansion on the outskirts of Cincinnati, people are firing at each other with bright yellow foam balls from a Nerf toy. Meanwhile, on the first floor, a Dixieland quartet is thumping out tunes. Within earshot, people are scribbling on purple index cards. What are they scribbling? Anything that comes to mind. Other folks in the mansion are being asked to talk about their worst vacation, and whether they have any scars and how they got them.

What the heck is going on here?

You have entered the twilight zone of America's idea industry. These are the creative mavens who promise to jump-start your business or energize old products through a sudden rush of—you guessed it—fresh ideas.

The problem is, the search for a new idea often gets subverted into a dizzying, Alice-in-Wonderland journey—with a lot of mumbo-jumbo about "creative emancipation," "mind pumping," and "mood morphing," not to mention a price tag that would make Alice blush. (Those brainstormers in the old mansion charge as much as $150,000 per visit.)

It's certainly true that new ideas drive businesses. They're the fuel for tomorrow's success. But is the process of finding a new idea really as complex as some would have you believe? Or has a basically simple process been made to appear complex?

Innovation has very little to do with genius. It has very little to do with inspiration.

"The myth is that an owner-entrepreneur can depend on a flash of genius," says Peter Drucker. "I have been working with owner-entrepreneurs for 40 years. The ones who depend on the flash of genius also go out like one."

Let's take an honest look at how the mind gets a new idea. It happens in three steps.

1. **Preparation.** You immerse yourself in the problem. You collect information, data, and opinions. You tell your brain to get to work.
2. **Incubation.** While you are busy doing other things, a part of your unconscious mind is swirling. Your brain juxtaposes ideas, blends characteristics, funnels ideas together.
3. **Illumination.** A new and reasonably complete idea surfaces (seemingly out of nowhere). Voilá! You've done it.

That's *what* happens. Exactly *how* it happens is another matter.

(In the comic strip *B.C.*, two characters are discussing this subject. *First guy*: "What's an idea?" *Second guy*: "An idea is an inspirational thought." *First guy*: "Where do they come from?" *Second guy*: "I haven't the slightest idea.")

We're never going to understand how it happens.

But we do know that Mr. Edison was absolutely correct. It's okay to borrow someone else's idea. "Make it a habit," he said, "to keep on the lookout for novel and interesting ideas that others have used successfully."

Leopoldo Fernandez Pujals did just that. A decade ago, as more Spanish women began entering the workforce, the Cuban-American marketer sensed Spain's growing appetite for fast food. So he invested $80,000 to start a pizza delivery service in Madrid. Now, TelePizza boasts $260 million in sales, employs 13,000 workers, and is in eight countries. Since going public on the Spanish bolsa in late 1996, TelePizza's shares have soared from 14 to 123, and its market cap now tops $1.3 billion. Says Pujals, a 50-year-old Vietnam War veteran: "More and more people are asking me: 'What's our secret?'" (We know your secret. You knocked off Domino's "home delivery" idea.)

Let's say you're an upscale hotel manager trying to keep up with the Marriotts and the Hyatts in the battle over room amenities. Don't take your staff off to a retreat to dream up new goodies. Instead, study what independent hotels are doing to charm their guests (like the Charles Hotel in Cambridge, MA, which has a children's story line built into the guest phone).

The simplest way to solve a problem is to borrow an existing idea. Military designers borrowed from Picasso's art to create better camouflage patterns for tanks.

The simplest way to invent a new product is to adapt an existing idea. The pop singer and composer Paul Simon was asked where he got the inspiration for "Bridge over Troubled Waters." He was brutally honest. He said he was carrying around two melodies in his head—a Bach chorale and a gospel tune from the Swan Silvertones—"and I just pieced them together."

The Museum of Paleontology at the University of California at Berkeley held a dinosaur body-parts sale. The museum asked contributors to sponsor parts of a Tyrannosaurus rex that had to be assembled. Donors' names would appear on a plaque at the museum. Prices ranged from $20 for a tailbone to $5000 for the skull and jaws. (In case you're wondering, there are 300 pieces in your average T-rex skeleton.)

The effort was a huge success. People bought dinosaur parts in their kids' names. Elementary schools held bake sales to sponsor a bone.

And where did this idea come from? It was borrowed. The fund drive was akin to an opera house selling individual seats to benefactors.

Speaking of good causes, have you ever been invited to a big charity dinner, but you really didn't want to attend? You didn't want to go through the hassle of getting a baby-sitter, renting a tuxedo, or sitting through the speeches.

We understand, said some smart folks in Florida. Here is their "non-invitation" invitation:

The annual Goodwill Industries dinner
will not be held this year at the Americana Hotel.
No cocktails will be served at 7 p.m.
No dinner will be served at 8 p.m.
The master of ceremonies will not be Art Linkletter.
The Rev. Norman Vincent Peale will not read the invocation.
The guest speaker will not be Dear Abby.
Stay home and have a restful evening.
But please send $50 per person or $100 per couple.

Did this scheme work? Like gangbusters.

In the years since, it has been adopted by other Goodwill chapters and by hospital charities. (Would it work for your favorite foundation? Go ahead. Borrow it.)

In the early 1900s, William Durant acquired 20 supplier companies under General Motors. He then brought the parts and accessories makers into the design process of a new automobile model right from the start. Sears, Roebuck copied Durant's system by buying minority interests in its suppliers as a way of gaining both control and cost advantages. In the early 1930s, London-based Marks & Spencer copied Sears. Later the Japanese studied and copied both Sears and Marks & Spencer. (Is there a lesson here for your business?)

Toys "R" Us was one of the first category killers. Others studied and applied the concept: Home Depot in hardware, Staples and OfficeMax in office supplies, PetsMart in pet food.

You can increase your odds of solving a problem by becoming a collector. When you come across a nifty notion or a savvy strategy, save it. Start a journal, a clipping file, and a computer file. Keep a pad by the bed, a voice recorder in the car.

When you're trying to find a solution to something, dip into your collection. Then use the following blueprint to make the most of an existing idea. (The blueprint itself is adapted from a checklist by Alex Osborn, author of *Applied Imagination*.)[17]

1. **Substitute.** What could you substitute in the approach, materials, ingredients, or appearance? SugarPops became CornPops, a more nutrition-conscious cereal. *Romeo and Juliet* begat *West Side Story*. Recently, the Hartford Ballet borrowed *The Nutcracker*, reset it in California in the 1800s, and added American Indians, Levi-Strauss, and Mark Twain. *The result*: Boffo reviews for *The American Nutcracker*.

2. **Combine.** What could you blend with an existing idea? What ingredients, appeals, colors, flavors? Lipton combined fruits and flavors with its tea to develop new iced teas.

3. **Adapt.** What else is this idea like? What could you copy? Sony adapted its Walkman concept into the Watchman TV and Discman CD. (This has been called the "managed evolution" of a product or process.) Gillette adapted its razor-innovation approach (Trac II, Atra, Sensor, Sensor Excel, etc.) to Oral-B toothbrushes. Oral-B hadn't introduced a new toothbrush in the 27 years before Gillette acquired it. Now Gillette has a team of 150 people researching manual plaque removal. And it has a stream of new products—from a floss made with a proprietary fiber to its top-of-the-line Advantage toothbrush.

4. **Magnify or Minimize.** What if you added, lengthened, strengthened, or subtracted? With sports utility vehicles selling like hotcakes, Ford upped the ante with the even bigger Expedition and the Lincoln Navigator. McDonald's is minimizing its outlets to fit inside airport terminals and retail locations like Home Depot.

5. **Put it to other uses.** What other ways could you use what you already have? Arm & Hammer transformed baking soda into a refrigerator deodorant, an underarm deodorant, and a toothpaste ingredient. Folks in Coatesville, PA, transformed an old

boarded-up hospital into a shelter for the homeless and apartments for low-income elderly.

6. **Eliminate.** What could you get rid of? Saturn set out to eliminate the fear and loathing of salespeople in the car-buying process.

7. **Reverse or rearrange.** What could you transpose or look at backward? Reverse the physics of a cold Thermos and you have a hot Thermos. Reverse your phone systems and you solve a customer problem. That's what happened at the headquarters of Meineke, the discount muffler people. Franchisees complained about never reaching a live voice, because their incoming toll-free calls were going into an automated answering system. A receptionist at the switchboard was answering local calls (mostly vendors and personal calls for employees). *Simple solution*: Switch the two systems.

Dale Carnegie, of *Win Friends and Influence People* fame, was a famous borrower. He once wrote: "The ideas I stand for are not mine. I borrowed them from Socrates. I swiped them from Chesterfield. I stole them from Jesus. And I put them in a book. If you don't like their rules, whose would you use?"

A SIMPLE SUMMATION

Show me someone else's idea.

CHAPTER 17

Goals

They sound nice but accomplish little

Some companies change what they're doing to get the future they want. This is a waste of time. You can get the same result by adjusting the assumptions in your business plan. Remember, the future depends on assumptions and the assumptions are just stuff you make up. No sense in knocking yourself out.

— Scott Adams,
The Dilbert Principle

Goals are responsible for mucking up marketing plans. We are opposed to them because they introduce unreality into the marketing process.

Managers who are obsessed with "what they want to do" love to set goals.

What are long-term plans except a meticulous outline of where managers want their company to be in five or ten years? The talk is of market share and return on equity goals.

These types of managers are trying to force things to happen instead of trying to find things to exploit. They tend to chase existing markets instead of looking for new opportunities. They also are internally oriented instead of being externally oriented.

When pressed about goals being nothing but wishful thinking, top managers tend to defend them as being "something to shoot at"—sort of a target. But what these people don't realize is that goal setting tends to communicate an unwillingness to accept failure. Because of this, people will fail to do the right things because they're busy trying to hit those unreal goals.

Trying to hit that mythical sales goal will encourage brand managers to push unnecessary line extensions or gin-up expensive promotions to load up distribution. But worse, it also keeps them from isolating the problem, facing it squarely, and then going all out to solve it.

We suspect that Cadillac's latest venture into a model that looks like a Chevrolet is driven by a goal of increasing Cadillac's share of the younger luxury car buyer who is very import oriented. Capturing the minds of this group is probably another goal that's not achievable. The impossible is impossible. You have to face reality.

Another problem with goal setting is that it creates a certain amount of inflexibility. When you're focused on a goal, you tend to miss opportunities that present themselves when you take a different direction.

While GM has been focused on the goal of increasing Cadillac's shrinking market, they have failed to see what could be done.

What has always been obvious was the opportunity for a new GM brand in the super-premium segment of the market. As it happens, GM already owns the perfect name. We would encourage GM to bring back the LaSalle. (For our younger readers, the LaSalle was one of the great classic cars of the twenties and thirties. Although part of the Cadillac family, the LaSalle was usually treated as a separate brand.)

The irony of bringing back the LaSalle brand to compete with the European cars is the fact that it was originally conceived as a car with a "European look." It was modeled after the French Hispano-Suiza, a car only the historians remember.

Today's version would obviously have to be smaller and quite expensive like the European sedans. And most important, it would have to be sold by a new breed of LaSalle dealers, not Cadillac dealers (in the same way that Acuras are sold by Acura dealers, not Honda dealers).

While this kind of tactic shift might have worked better years ago, it still is the only move GM can make today if it wants a larger share of the super-premium segment. At those prices, who wouldn't want a larger piece?

In the very popular book *Built to Last*, James Collins and Jerry Porras talk glowingly about "Big Hairy Audacious Goals." They claim that it's these goals that have helped turn companies like Boeing, Wal-Mart, General Electric, IBM, Philip Morris, and others into the successful giants they have become.

But if you look closely at their thesis, "goals" are mixed up with "bold moves."

Boeing's bet on the first commercial jet aircraft (the 707) was a bold move not a goal. It enabled Boeing to be first.

IBM's bet on the 360 was a bold, new-generation-of-computers move. Leaders stay leaders by, in some instances, competing with themselves.

Citicorp's goal of making the bank a big domestic and international financial institution was also about establishing leadership in the early stages of big-time banking.

The authors of *Built to Last* give examples of companies that were founded from 1812 (Citicorp) to 1945 (Wal-Mart). They didn't have to deal with the intense competition in today's global economy. While there is much to be learned from the success of these companies, you must realize that they had the luxury of growing up in a time when business life was a lot simpler.

A SIMPLE SUMMATION

Goals are like dreams. Wake up and face reality.

CHAPTER 18

Growth

It can be bad for your business

We don't have a desperate need to grow.
We have a desperate desire to grow.

— Milton Friedman

Growth is the by-product of doing things right. But in itself it is not a worthy goal. In fact, growth is the culprit behind impossible goals.

CEOs pursue growth to ensure their tenures and to increase their take home pay. Wall Street brokers pursue growth to ensure their reputations and to increase their take-home pay.

To us a simpler and more powerful objective is to shoot for share, not profits. As a market emerges, your number one objective should be to establish a dominant market share. Too many companies want to take profits before they have consolidated their position.

What makes a company strong is not the product or the service. It's the position it owns in the mind. The strength of Hertz is in its leadership position, not the quality of its rent-a-car service. It's easier to stay on top than to get there.

Can you name a company that has overturned a leader? Crest did it in toothpaste, thanks to the American Dental Association's seal of approval. (Ironically, Colgate has regained the lead with its germ-killing Total toothpaste.) Duracell did it in batteries thanks to "Alkaline." Budweiser did it in beer, and Marlboro did it in cigarettes. But it rarely happens.

A survey of 25 leading brands from the year 1923 proves this point. Today, 20 of those brands are still in first place. Four are in second place, and one is in fifth place.

Even changes in rank don't happen very often. If marketing were a horse race, it would be a deadly dull affair. In the 56 years since World War II, there has been only one change in position in the top three U.S. automobile companies.

In 1950 Ford Motor Company moved past Chrysler Corporation into second place. Since then the order has been General Motors, Ford, Chrysler all the way. Monotonous, isn't it?

The "stickiness" of a marketing race, the tendency for companies or brands to remain in the same position year after year, also underscores the importance of securing a good position in the first place. Improving your position might be difficult, but once you do, it becomes relatively easy to maintain that new position.

When you do get on top, make sure the marketplace knows it. Too many companies take their leadership for granted and never exploit it. All this does is keep the door open for competition. If you get the chance, slam the door in your competition's face. Americans loves the underdog, but they prefer to buy from the overdogs.

Such was the case in rayon viscose fiber. In terms of sales it's a market that's evenly divided among an Austrian company (Lenzing), a U.K. company (Courtaulds), a company in India (Biria), and one in China.

But Lenzing had the best technological credentials, a technology that it has been working at since 1930. That set up its program to build the industry perception of being the world leader in rayon viscose technology. Lenzing told the story of how, thanks to it, rayon is a fiber that just gets better. It was preempting leadership.

Never finance the company's losers with the earnings from the company's winners, which is a typical accounting trick in a multiproduct company. This dampens your ability to pour on the resources to your winners.

But because of Wall Street pressure, many companies stay focused on growth and miss the opportunity to pour it on. Or better said, they become distracted.

Consider the current saga of Silicon Graphics. This is the workstation company that brought you visual computing and all those wonderful graphics that Hollywood produces. And with the acquisition of Cray Supercomputers, it currently is the world leader in high-performance computers.

But instead of pouring on the resources and preempting its "high-performance" differentiating idea, it is under Wall Street pressure to broaden its business. To those analysts, high-performance computing is a niche, and not up to a 20 percent per annum growth.

When you're the Porsche of computers, you don't move into cheaper computers. You dominate the high-performance business by getting more customers to want high-performance computing. (After all, what wealthy company wants low performance computing?)

You can't let Wall Street drive your business.

Most financial moguls have a mathematical approach to marketing. The more businesses they're in, the faster they figure the businesses will grow. Consider the current saga of Nike. When the world goes out to play, Nike wants to outfit it from head to toe. And it is even looking at supplying the equipment with which we play as its design teams take their high-tech approach to bats, balls and gloves.

The obvious strategy is to make Nike a sports "megabrand." The company's tactic is to put its swoosh logo on every big sports team and big sports name it can buy. Even TV announcers at the last Winter Olympics were spotted with a swoosh on their jackets. (Nike founder Phil Knight is never without his logo. He has a swoosh tattoo.) Whatever the game, Nike wants to do it.

But of late, the world doesn't seem to want to play. A glance at some Nike articles in the recent magazines and newspapers tells the story:

"Teens Give Boot to Nike" (*U.S. News & World Report*)[18] talks about young adults abandoning pricey Nike sneakers. "Tripped by Too Many Shoes, Nike Regroups" (*The Wall Street Journal*)[19] presents the problems of dreaming up 350 new sneaker models every year. "Nike Shows Feet of Clay: Cutbacks Ahead" (*Footwear News*)[20] writes about reduced earnings and potential layoffs. "Just Do It without Nike" (*Discount Store News*)[21] lays out the need for stores to have more brands than just Nikes.

What's going on here? Why is Nike no longer cool?

Josephine Esquivel, an analyst at Morgan Stanley, had it right when she said, "Nike's biggest problem is the over-Swooshing of America."

In the effort to pursue "endless growth" Nike has fallen into what we call the line-extension trap. It's typical megabrand thinking where you hang your brand on as many related or even nonrelated categories as possible. It's what we call "inside" thinking about a successful brand and how to make it bigger and better.

Unfortunately, the only thinking that works in the marketplace is the "outside" thinking that works in the mind of the prospect. Consider what happened to these big brands:

- Chevrolet was once the best-selling family car. Now a Chevrolet is a big, small, expensive, cheap, sedan, sports car, van, or truck that is outsold by Ford, Honda, and Toyota.

- Xerox spent 20 years and several billion dollars trying to be a company offering copiers to computers and everything in-between. It finally realized that any Xerox machine that couldn't make a copy was in trouble.

- McDonald's built a widely successful business on inexpensive, high-speed hamburgers. But then it wanted to became more of a restaurant that offered kids hamburgers, grown-up hamburgers, pizza, chicken, you name it. Now it has become slower and much less successful. It was a "Mc" too far.

- Marlboro suffered a market share loss when it got carried away with Regulars, Lights, Ultra-lights, Mediums, and Menthol cigarettes. Finally it began to realize that real cowboys don't smoke Mediums, Menthols, and Ultra-lights. It went back to Marlboro Country and things got better.

As we said in Chapter 7, in business it's differentiate, differentiate, differentiate. The more things you try to become and the more you lose focus, the more difficult it is to differentiate your product.

People don't buy you because you're a megabrand. In the world of games, people buy the best brand of sneakers or golf balls or tennis rackets or whatever. They buy what they think offers them the most of what they want. And more times than not, they buy the specialist in that category. *The reason:* If a company specializes, it must know how to make it better than the nonspecialist.

Tiger Woods has a multimillion dollar reason to wear Nike from head to toe. But the rest of us have no reason. The sooner that Nike realizes that it's not about logos but about differentiated products, the sooner its game will improve.

Trying to be all things to all people is complicated and wasteful. That strategy fritters away resources on side battles, resources that ought to be concentrated on the main event. Decisions are a lot simpler when you've got one thing on which to focus.

In our experience, less is more.

Subaru was a pioneer in all-wheel drive (AWD). Back in the 1970s, it built a strong brand image for offbeat, rugged vehicles that performed in snow and mud.

However the company nearly went bankrupt in the 1980s when it left that foul-weather image and challenged Honda, Nissan, and Toyota in the mainstream car business. Subaru produced a big lineup of sedans and sports cars. By 1993, Subaru had lost money for seven years in a row—a total of $750 million.

Then the company scrapped loser lines, streamlined, and returned to its AWD roots. By 1996, it was only doing 64 percent of the volume it had a decade earlier. But by 1996, it was back in the black.

Less can be more in any business. Amorim, a Portuguese company, is the world leader in wine corks. Krones AG, a German company, has a 70 percent worldwide market share of the machines that put labels on beverage bottles. The Spanish manufacturing company Chupa Chips decided in 1957 to discontinue some 200 products and focus on one—lollipops. It now dominates the world market.

A true story illustrates where the love of growth is at the root of evil doings.

We were brought in to evaluate business plans for a large multi-brand drug company. In turn, the brand managers stood up and presented their next year's plans.

In the course of a presentation, a young executive warned of aggressive new competition in his category that would definitely change the balance of power. But when it came to sales projection, there was a predicted 15 percent increase. Instantly we questioned how this could be with the new competition.

His answer was that they were going to do some short-term maneuvering and line extension. Wouldn't this hurt the long-term strategy? Well, yes. Then why do it? Because his boss made him put in the increase and you'll have to talk with him.

One week later, the boss admitted the problem but said his boss needed the increase because of, you guessed it, Wall Street.

A SIMPLE SUMMATION

Build market share and the numbers will come.

People Issues

Business is all about highly trained, skilled people.
Try not to confuse them with nonsense.

CHAPTER 19

Motivation

Effort alone is not the answer

To change and to improve are two different things.
— *German proverb*

A national magazine called in a top-flight trainer. Advertising sales were drooping. Morale was flagging. Would she come to the next sales meeting and speak?

Before saying yes, she did her homework. The magazine's name and reputation were old-fashioned. It had gone through cosmetic redesigns. Its editorial content was unfocused and confusing. There was considerable resistance among ad space buyers.

Her diagnosis: No real strategy, no clear point of differentiation. She'd be glad to address these important issues.

The publisher's response: "Oh, we're really just looking for a motivational speech. We need to recharge people, get them moving again."

Folks, effort alone is not the answer. Trying harder is overblown.

Motivating your employees is not going to hardwire them to the corporate core—especially because they've probably already figured out that job security is a thing of the past. Wave after wave of mergers, downsizings, and restructurings haven't helped much on the loyalty front. The fragile bond between organization and employee has snapped. The attitude of many workers is, "We're all essentially temps."

Yet motivation is such a tempting solution. As management counselor Alan Weiss reports, "I don't know how many times I've heard executives deliver the admonition, 'We can't rest on our laurels. We have to work even harder from here.'"

So someone has a bright idea: Let's give the troops a little R&R. We'll send them off to a motivational rally, where they be inspired by catchy slogans. Here are some slogans that filled the air at one such festival:

- "Feel like a champ and you'll be a champ."
- "Winners don't give up. They get up."
- "Success doesn't come overnight. It comes over time."

Or you might decide to bring a motivational speaker right into the company's auditorium. There the charismatic he or she can inspire the troops to "be all you can be" and to "ignite your booster engines" (all this accompanied by balloons and buttons and booklets.) These talks have titles such as:

- "Big Things Happen When You Do the Little Things Right"
- "The Fine Art of Getting Extra Effort from Everyone"
- "100 Ways to Motivate Yourself"
- "1,001 Ways to Motivate Yourself and Others" (Obviously, 100 is for amateurs.)

Or you could go big time and bring in a big-name motivator.

Andersen Consulting hired General, Colin Powell at $60,000 to speak to an internal meeting of senior managers, where the good general radiated authority and confidence.

"He really held the audience with his anecdotes about the Gulf War and his personal life," says the Andersen chieftain who arranged things. "However, he said nothing that pertained to the meeting. I knew he wouldn't know enough about Andersen's business to provide insight to what our people are doing. That wasn't the objective." (Then what was the objective?)

Money, of course, is one objective. Motivation is serious business. The speaking part of it alone generated $1 billion in annual revenues, according to one training magazine. (Balloons are extra.)

Do powerful outside speakers add real value? Or do they just fog the minds of already-confused employees?

Let's apply some common sense to the extra-effort crowd. Behind most such efforts, there is misguided reasoning. It goes like this: Give the troops something special, whip them into a lather, and they'll try harder, sell more, and produce more. They'll go the extra mile.

You know what? It never happens. For one thing, this stuff may feel great, but the effect evaporates in minutes. It's just a mental massage.

It's just entertainment. For another thing, what do you think happens when the "effort doctor" packs up and leaves your building? Of course. He's on to the next auditorium to deliver the identical "yes-you-can" message to the next crowd—probably to your competitors.

Remember, every company has access to the same psychology, the same speakers, the same pep rallies.

Don't misunderstand us. There's nothing wrong with the concept of wanting to motivate someone. As Will Rogers once said in his understated way: "Even if you're on the right track, you'll get run over if you just sit there."

But first make sure you're on the right track. Make certain that you know where you want your people to go and that they have the fundamental training and tools to get there.

Go back to the basics for a minute. What's the dictionary definition of "motivate?" *Answer:* "To move someone to action." What specific action do you have in mind? What exactly do you want listeners to do?

The question the folks in the auditorium need answered is not, "How do I unlock my true potential?" The question they need answered is, "What makes this company different?" (What's the idea I can latch onto and run with?) This puts real demands on the guy at the front of the room.

The most effective motivational speeches come from someone inside the company, someone who's been down to the front lines and came back to give an honest report. And these days, leading the charge demands the ability to be passionate and articulate about the company's strategy. (See Chapter 12 on leadership.)

We were once in the audience when the CEO of a $100 billion global bank took the stage. Hundreds of crisply pressed suits leaned forward, awaiting *the word*. The CEO cleared his throat and said: "Our overriding objective is to provide quality products to quality clients in quality markets around the world."

Is there a competitive idea there? Is there a mental angle there?

Platitudes do not a difference make. In fact, they do damage to today's skeptical and suspicious workers by raising false expectations.

What that CEO should be delivering is a platform of ideas on "how we're going to kick butt," followed by "here are the tools to do it with."

Real motivation starts with the weapon of an idea, and then a challenge to the troops to bring it to life in sales, product development, engineering, whatever. Real motivation is about doing battle in the real world, not in the feel-good land of "peak performance."

A SIMPLE SUMMATION

Working harder is not as effective as working smarter.

CHAPTER 20

Self-improvement

It's the emperor's new clothes

Evolution implies getting better and better in every way, ultimately getting for ourselves the best of everything.

—Deepak Chopra,
Self-improvement spiritualist

Once upon a time, an employee's karma was his or her own business. But more and more, companies are tackling the spiritual aspects of employees.

The goal is to create more centered employees who prosper in a holistic and emotionally tranquil environment. No snickering, please. These new age mantras are sweeping over the landscape faster than El Niño. "Inner child" and "human potential" are now part of the standard business vocabulary.

American business spends $15 billion each year on all forms of employee training. The fastest-growing segment? Personal transformation and self-improvement. Management theory has now locked arms with self-help, oriental philosophy, futurology, and outright quackery.

Do your employees have wounded psyches? There is a cure for whatever ails them.

- Boeing Company gathered top managers and had them tell stories of their time to date with the company. Then they put the negative parts in writing and burned them in a ritual act of corporate death and rebirth.

- In a program at California's Esalen Institute titled "Ending the Fractured Self," rituals and ceremonies focus on "release and renewal." (Participants are asked to bring a bandanna, a journal, drums, and rattles.)

You might think that's a bit unusual. Well, read on.

- A training group in New Mexico uses concepts and perception-altering exercises drawn from Navajo and Apache traditions. Clients such as Honeywell and Bethlehem Steel send people off to study the Medicine Wheel—a representation of the four poles of human experience (intellectual, physical, emotional, and spiritual).

- Participants in another learning lab design a "touchstone" from wood, rocks, fabrics, leaves, and bits of glass. They use these "to symbolize what their job means to them." Later in the process, they may actually redesign their touchstones. (I'll see your two rocks and raise you one.)

New age thinking has even filtered into MBA programs and into the White House.

- A Georgetown University business school professor requires his students to go out on campus in broad daylight and scream at the top of their lungs. "Sometimes," he says, "I have students pretend they're a bowl of Jell-O, or pizza, or I have them bark like a dog."
- Jean Houston, a founder of the "human potential" movement and a confidante of Hillary Clinton, recommends exercises to "recover the self." Participants remove their shoes, rings, and glasses. They sit in two circles, back to back, with arms linked and eyes closed, and sing. This is known as "the remembrance of the primal community."
- The Clintons are also raving fans of personal transformation people like Stephen Covey and Tony Robbins. (More on them shortly.)

Drums and rattles? Touchstones and meditation? Barking like a dog? Will future captains of industry really be packing tarot cards and chants to go along with their laptops?

To answer those questions, we need to take a closer look at Covey, Chopra, and Robbins—the Big Three rivals in the business of selling the self to the businessperson.

Stephen Covey stands for the new American dream—economic success and spiritual salvation in one package. *USA Today* calls him "the hottest self-improvement consultant to hit U.S. business since Dale Carnegie." His training business, founded in 1985 with two employees, now has 700 people and revenues of $100 million. Clients include half the Fortune 500 companies and thousands of smaller organizations.

His first book, *The 7 Habits of Highly Effective People*, has sold 10 million copies. *Message:* To reach your full potential, you have to build character.

Stephen Covey does not tell us what to do. He tells us how to reach inside ourselves, find the right universal principle, and apply it.

Seven such principles exist in his world (no more, no less). One of them, the win-win principle, is an interesting study. Covey says he will tell us all we need to know to be effective, but he also promises to tell everyone else as well. So your competitors will know what you know. Not to worry, says Professor Covey. If we all know what we have all known all along, we will all be better off. (Give us a ring when you figure that out.)

Even so, it's hard to doubt Covey's sincerity. He is a lifelong and unflinching Mormon. With a Harvard MBA, a doctorate in organizational behavior, and 20 years of teaching business management, he is no fanatic.

But these are just old bromides, say his critics. Work hard. Follow the golden rule. You must/ought/should plan ahead. So why all the hype?

Covey is practicing "White Magic," says Alan Wolfe in *The New Republic:*[22] "Its goal is to persuade people that things which are perfectly obvious, even completely known to them, can nonetheless be revealed to them."

Deepak Chopra is a former Boston endocrinologist, born and raised in New Delhi, educated for 12 years by Jesuit missionaries. Today, he is a self-described "pioneer in the field of mind-body medicine and human potential."

His enterprises bring in at least $15 million a year. He's very big with middle-aged professionals. There are 19 books, a monthly news-letter, $25,000 lectures, and five-day seminars.

The message of Deepak Chopra is a bouillabaisse of eastern philos-ophy, western theology, Celtic traditions, modern medicine, and even rap music. "Everything he's ever heard is grist for his mill, " says one observer.

Millions of his fervent believers swear by his message, even though they can't explain exactly what that message is. No wonder, when you plunge into *The 7 Spiritual Laws of Success* and find this incantation: "Life is the eternal dance of consciousness that expresses itself as the dynamic exchange of impulses of intelligence between microcosm and macrocosm, between the human body and the universal body, between the human mind and the cosmic mind."

We decided to sample a Deepak Chopra book and tape offering titled *Creating Affluence*. First came this note from the author: "This material is extremely concentrated and has to be literally metabolized and experienced in the consciousness." (We chewed hard and swal-lowed.)

Soon we were learning that: "People with wealth consciousness settle only for the best. This is also called the principle of highest first. Go first class all the way and the universe will respond by giving you the best." (If you go first class from New York to Los Angeles, the universe tends to respond with a bill for $3688.)

At a lecture series billed as "The Journey to the Boundless," Chopra tells the audience: "We're going to explore the mechanics of the mirac-ulous and the spontaneous fulfillment of your desires."

Wait a minute. There do seem to be boundaries to the boundless journey. An apostle tells the audience about the "Seduction of the Spirit" seminar to be held later that same year. Sign up now, and save $400.

Like his self-help brethren, Chopra is a brilliant marketing machine. Outside that hotel ballroom, his machine sells books, tapes, herbal teas, vitamins, and massage oils.

Any why not? "Spirituality and wealth consciousness go hand-in-hand," according to Chopra. "Poverty is a reflection of an impoverished spirit."

Tony Robbins is a jut-jawed, Armani-suited warrior, 6-foot, 7-inches tall, who strides onstage to exploding smoke machines and strobe lights.

A bright kid with bad acne who left home at age 17, Robbins is now a 40-year-old "peak performer" who makes millions a year from his adrenaline-fueled seminars. His "personal power" TV infomercials have sold tens of millions of self-help tapes. He's very big with 25-year-old males on the career track. He divides his time between a castle in San Diego (with helicopter pad) and an island in the South Pacific.

The essence of Robbins's message, laid down in books such as *Awaken the Giant Within* and *Unlimited Power*, is that you can achieve anything you want just as long as you adopt the right attitude. (Think it and it will be yours.)

"I want to make sure that you make a commitment to a life of constant and never-ending improvement," he says in his seminars. (You can start by grabbing a few more tapes on your way out.)

Tony Robbins found fame when he stumbled across a little-known (and highly suspect) therapeutic technique called neurolinguistic programming (NLP). NLP uses a light-trance hypnosis to rewire the subconscious mind, supposedly eliminating painful phobias, negative self-image, and other problems.

By learning what to think and how to hold his body, Robbins found he could walk barefoot through a bed of coals burning at 2000 degrees. He called his fire walk the mind revolution. "If you can make yourself walk through fire," he yells at his audiences, "what can't you do?" An empire was born.

People like Tony Robbins are the scalawags in the field, says Adrian Wooldridge, a bureau chief for *The Economist* and coauthor of *The Witch Doctors*, a valuable book that dissects management counselors and gurus.

"Tony Robbins is selling hope and credulity," Wooldridge told *Training Magazine*, "the idea that if you just change your attitude about the world you unleash this fantastic amount of power and you become a successful person without effort. It's just nonsense. He's selling faint hope to suckers."[23]

We think it's time to "stop the insanity," to quote the title of another faddish self-help program. Here is some simple advice to deal with self-improvement issues.

1. **Understand what's going on here.** It starts with insecure or unhappy people. Offer them an answer to their problem. Cloak the advice in language that seems intelligent but is mostly gibberish. Acknowledge that the world is troubled, but demand very few changes in the way they actually live and work.

   "The spiritual peace and enlightenment offered by pop gurus doesn't require a lifetime of discipline," says Wendy Kaminer, a commentator on National Public Radio. "It requires that you suspend your critical judgment, attend their lectures and workshops and buy their books or tapes."

   Forbes magazine calls them the "happiness hucksters."

   In their book *We've Had a Hundred Years of Psychotherapy and the World's Getting Worse*, James Hillman and Michael Venture explain the feebleness of new age enlightenment. "It's the cultivation of the inner landscape at the expense of the outer world," they say. "What you learn is mainly feeling skills. But you don't find out anything about the way the world works."

2. **Leave personal growth to the person.** If your people want to walk on hot coals and bang drums, let them do it on their own time. And with their own dollars. It's probably a harmless addiction, no more dangerous than caffeine. In the meantime,

put the company's training dollars into efforts that produce better workers, not better souls.

3. **Start by improving the basics.** Take an honest look at your workforce. Chances are, you've got people who don't read well, don't speak well, can't compose a coherent memo, can't read a balance sheet, can't turn on a computer. That's where to start the training.

"People have to be trained for exactly what they really do," says retired Navy Commander Richard Marcinko, who now heads a private security firm. For example, the training of the FedEx workforce focuses on the single, primary vision that created the company in the first place: overnight delivery. FedEx has trained its workers to ship and track packages so efficiently that the U.S. Army, in designing he supply system for the Gulf War, copied the training techniques of FedEx.

4. **After the basics, work on skill building.** That's the approach the serious players take.

In 1995 Motorola spent $150 million on corporate education, offering at least 40 hours of training to each of its 132,000 workers. General Electric spends more than $500 million annually on training and runs a world-class Leadership Development Center in Crotonville, NY.

Companies of any size can learn from the GE model. GE started by reviewing existing theories on training and other companies' best practices. The result was a nucleus of a course that 1100 top managers took over seven days. That, in turn, became a spring-board for managers to take information into the field to train tens of thousands of other managers and workers.

"You never send a changed person back to an unchanged environment," says the director of GE's training programs. "That's Organizational Development 101."

5. **Remember, it's called training, not recreation.** A seminar shouldn't be as dull as C-Span. But watch out for any program where business-people dress up as druids and witches and go off on mythical quests. Let's give the last word to Tony Robbins. At a certain point in his seminars, Mr. Robbins is reported to stand up and shout, "We're going to feel good today for no reason at all."

We rest our case.

A SIMPLE SUMMATION

There's a sucker born every day, and two to sell them.

CHAPTER 21

Success

It's about finding a horse to ride

Life is a cobweb. The lines cross at funny angles. Whether you're successful or not doesn't depend on how good your plans are, especially those five-year strategic plans business schools teach. Success depends on how you react to unexpected opportunities.

— Ross Perot

To be successful today, there is only one simple approach: View yourself as a product rather than as an employee. Your career is in your own hands, not in the hands of your smiling head of human resources.

Trying harder, believing in yourself, walking on fire, and saying "yes I can" are not steps up the ladder of success. The surprising truth is that success does not spring from anything inside yourself at all. Success is something given to you by others.

When you focus on yourself, you have only one ticket on the race. By expanding your horizon to include others, you greatly increase the odds in your favor.

In other words, success is finding a horse to ride. And you only find that horse when you shrug off your preoccupation with your inner self—when you open your mind to the outside world, when you search for success outside of yourself.

The good news is, success is all around you.

We've studied success and successful people. Once we got past their self-serving comments about "trying harder" and "sticking to a plan," we found out what really determines success. They all had horses to ride. Ideas, companies, mentors, and family.

Based on this study, here's some advice on where to look and what to look for—and which horse to ride. We'll even rate them for you.

The *hard-work horse* is the longest of the long shots. When you build your personal marketing strategy around your own talents and abilities and neglect outsiders, you are riding only yourself (After you put in 18 hours a day, you've got nothing left to give.)

The *IQ horse* is also a long shot. In the dairy, cream rises to the top. In daily life, it's generally not true. It's mostly skim milk at the top of the corporate bottle. You'd be appalled if you gave IQ tests to the CEOs of the Fortune 500 companies. (The professors at any decent community college would score higher.)

But the IQ horse can pay off. Such was the case of General George Marshall of Marshall Plan fame. He was brilliant and a man of great character. His intelligence was recognized by FDR, and he rode to the top of the army.

Surprisingly, the *company horse* is a long shot too. In the past, this was the horse to ride. A college-graduate-to-be would aim for the biggest company or the highest starting salary, preferably both. Once that decision was made, it was onward and upward. You were set for life. Today, the only time to ride the company horse is early. (Like people, companies tend to get tired and inflexible as they age.)

Companies like Xerox, Apple, and Microsoft spawned a pack of millionaires among their early hires. The pickings were slim for later arrivals. How do you spot a megacorporation in its infancy? You don't. You look for another person, a product, or an idea that seems to have a future.

On a personal level, the *hobby horse* is a medium shot. What you do on vacation and what you do as a vocation can be the same thing. Look at what Hugh Hefner accomplished without leaving his bedroom. Paul Prudhomme loves to eat, and his 500 pounds prove it. So he turned his hobby into the world-famous K-Paul's Kitchen in New Orleans. Paul and Nina Zagat turned their love of eating and traveling into a mini-empire of restaurant and travel guides across the United States.

The short shots are your best bets, like the *product horse*. The best example of riding a product horse to the top is Lee Iacocca. He had been fired by Henry Ford as president of Ford and went on to become a living legend at Chrysler. But how did Iacocca get to be president of Ford? In a word, Mustang. The Mustang was the horse Iacocca rode to the top. Did he design it? No. Did he engineer it? No. Did he recognize the merits of somebody else's design? Yes.

The brothers Dick and Mac McDonald opened their drive-in hamburger joint in 1948. Ray Kroc arrived on the scene five years later. Fame and fortune went to the recognizer of the concept, not the inventors.

A century before, Levi Strauss arrived in San Francisco with bolts of cloth to manufacture tents for miners in the gold rush. But he quickly saw they had enough tents. What prospectors needed the most were pants strong enough to withstand the rigors of the diggings. Levi Strauss found his gold by cutting trousers out of his tent cloth. (He used rivets on the pockets because that's the way tents were made.)

A fellow named Mike Markkula hitched a ride on the product horse named Apple. Because he liked what he saw in the Steve Jobs–Steve Wozniak garage, Mike Markkula put up $91,000 for a one-third interest in the fledgling company. He helped Steve Jobs write the business plan. He obtained a line of credit for Apple at the Bank of America. He was older and more experienced, but he chose to be a cooperator, not a competitor.

The *idea horse* is another good horse to ride. George de Maestral took a walk in the woods outside Geneva, Switzerland, and came back with cockleburs stuck to his jacket. Under a microscope, he found the burrs were covered with tiny hooks, which became snared in the fabric loops of his jacket. He saw a way to capitalize on his observation. (Chapter 16 describes the different ways to adapt an idea.) His curiosity led to Velcro, which also fastens with tiny hooks and loops.

How do you recognize a good idea? Here are some guidelines.

> Is it bold? Whenever you see a successful business, it means someone once made a courageous decision.
>
> Is it obvious? If it's obvious to your team, it will also be obvious to the marketplace, which means it will work that much faster. (ATMs were not a new idea when John Reed of Citicorp brought them to New York City.)
>
> Is it likely to upset the apple cart? Good ideas often have a strong competitive angle (the way Anita Roddick's Body Shops shook up the cosmetic industry).

The *other-person horse* is the best of all. The other person could be your boss, or an associate. Most people who work together see their associates as competitors, not potential collaborators. That's a shame. You have much more to gain by looking at the people around you as potential horses.

The other person could be a friend. Bill Gates and Paul Allen became buddies in the science lab at a Seattle prep school.

He or she could be a mentor. Randall Jay Moore learned about elephants from a circus animal trainer. Then he inherited three adult African beasts when his mentor died. Today, Mr. Moore runs the world's most exclusive elephant safari company on 500,000 acres in Botswana. (You might say, he found an elephant to ride.)

He or she could be a partner. The give-and-take atmosphere of a partnership allows ideas to be refined and perfected. *Cases in points:* Rogers and Hart; Simon and Garfunkel; Sonny and Cher Siskel and Ebert.

Or the other-person horse could be a parent or relative. There are 15 million businesses in America, and almost 90 percent are family-controlled or have a major family involvement. They range from mom-and-pop operations to some of the giants (Anheuser Busch, Mars, and Marriott, to name a few).

Too many people walk away from the family horse. "I can do it on my own," they say. Everybody needs a horse to ride. Why get off the horse you were born with?

Finally, some thoughts about "career planning."

One of the great myths in corporate America is career planning. Young people envision a land of mentors and managers, carefully guiding their steps up the ladder. As they rise, they are nurtured, trained, loved, and promoted.

Forget it. No one knows the future. Predicting the future is an exercise in delusion.

> Career planning at Wang became a little tricky when the PC overtook the word processor and pushed the company to the edge of disaster.

Career planning at General Foods soured when Philip Morris bought the company.

Career planning at MCI fizzled when the hotshots from Worldcom showed up.

Your best bet is to find a horse and cling to it for all you're worth. Riding is better than planning.

A SIMPLE SUMMATION

You don't find success inside yourself. You find success outside yourself.

CHAPTER 22

The critics

Being simple will not be easy

How much easier it is to be critical than to be correct.

— Benjamin Disraeli

As we said earlier, humans admire complexity even though they don't understand it. And because of the "Simple Simon factor," you run the risk of being ridiculed in your efforts to be simple—especially by the complexity crowd that is either selling complexity or hiding behind it to avoid making decisions.

Your critics' comments will come in a number of different forms, so you should stand ready to defend yourself. Here are their favorite critiques.

1. **You will be called "simplistic."** They will say that you are being excessively simple and that a more ingenious answer is needed. How could something that simple work? Here you look them in the eye and quote Thomas Hazlitt, the British essayist: "Simplicity of character is the natural result of profound thought."

2. **You will be accused of "not understanding."** They will say that this is a problem that is so complex that it obviously must require a complex solution. You just don't understand all the nuances. Here you quote Winston Churchill: "Out of intense complexities, intense simplicities emerge."

3. **You will be told "we know all that."** Your simple answers will be declared too obvious and basic. What they will demand are the alternatives. There must be an unknown answer to the problem, something of which no one has thought. Here you wheel in Henri Deterding, director general of Royal Dutch Oil: "Whenever I have met a business proposition which, after taking thought, I could not reduce to simplicity, I have left it alone."

4. **You will be charged with being "lazy."** Here you will be criticized for not supplying all that extra thinking and supporting

data. Their premise is that if it looks complex, it took far more effort than a simple approach that lacks detail. Here you tell your critics what Edward Teller, the famous physicist, advised: "To pursue simplicity in life, in the world, in the future, is a most valuable enterprise."

Have courage. When you pursue simplicity you are on the side of the world's leading thinkers. Albert Einstein, one of the best, put it this way: "Possessions, outward success, publicity, luxury—to me these have always been contemptible. I believe that a simple and unassuming manner of life is best for every one, best both for the body and the mind."

A SIMPLE SUMMATION

The best revenge over critics is being correct.

In Conclusion

Don't get us wrong. Not everyone is into "complexity." Those who are practicing simplicity are doing very well, thank you.

CHAPTER 23

Simplicity

Its power is alive and well

Nothing is more simple than greatness; indeed, to be simple is to be great.

— Ralph Waldo Emerson

When we started this book, we talked mostly about the evils of complexity and how it can get in the way of doing the right thing. We would like to end with the thought that simplicity is at the heart of many success stories in business. Some we've already touched on such as Procter & Gamble, and some we haven't.

Here's a cross-section of different companies in different businesses that are using the power of simplicity.

Papa John's Pizza. We wrote earlier about John's success in the pizza category. This success has resulted in *Restaurants & Institutions* magazine voting this organization as the "Best Pizza Chain in America" for two years running.

When we asked the founder, John Schnatter, about this success, here's what he had to say:

> "There are no secrets to our success. It's all about better ingredients and quality and good old fashioned hard work. The biggest thing we do differently is that we keep things simple. It's not that we don't know how to make complex pizza such as Sicilian pizza, deep-dish pizza and stuffed crust pizza. But thirteen years ago we simply decided to make a better traditional pizza. We now make that product better than anybody does in the world. To reach that level of expertise, we had to give up some other products. We also keep other things simple. Every commissary has the same mixer, the same water purification system, the same oven, and even the same computer. This keeps our quality continuous and avoids errors."

In just 13 years, that simple approach has generated almost $900 million in annual sales.

The power of simplicity.

Chick-fil-A. This chicken restaurant also found success in fast food land with a simple idea. "We didn't invent the chicken," the ads say. "Just the chicken sandwich."

Chick-fil-A's premium chicken sandwich is served the same way it was 35 years ago. New products are seldom introduced. There are no "limited time" special deals.

Outnumbered and outspent six to one by the likes of McDonald's, Burger King, and Wendy's, Chick-fil-A is now selling $750 million worth of just chicken sandwiches.

The power of simplicity.

Southwest Airlines. Herb Kelleher has built what has turned out to be one of America's most profitable and successful airlines. The airline was founded on the premise of keeping things simple. First there was only one kind of airplane, the Boeing 737. That made things simpler for the pilots and the maintenance people.

Then there were no assigned seats, just reusable plastic boarding passes. That meant no groping for seats. No boarding a halfhour early. And better yet, no overbooking. At Southwest, you come on and the plane takes off. You save time. It arrives on time.

There was no lousy food—as a matter of fact, no food at all. Besides, what you save on Southwest, you can spend at a gourmet restaurant when you arrive. Also, there's no waiting at the gate while the food is being loaded on board.

There are no hubs. The planes fly direct to where you want to go, not where Southwest wants you to change planes. The planes fly the shortest distance between two points. It's quicker that way. The company saves fuel, and so it can charge less.

Southwest avoids O'Hare, Dallas/Ft. Worth, and all the giant airports where you can spend an hour finding your gate. Easy on, easy off is the airline's philosophy.

When asked about the company's dedication to simplicity, Herb tells this story:

"When Southwest started in 1971, we used cash register tickets that looked and felt very much like bus tickets. Customers wrote and complained that: 1. They threw them in the trash by accident because of their insignificant appearance; 2. Their pets ate them; 3. They washed them into oblivion with their jeans. A proposal was made to install a multi-million dollar computerized ticketing system to rectify the problems. During the discussion, one of our vice presidents suggested that we simply modify the cash register machines to print "THIS IS A TICKET" across the top of each piece of paper issued by the cash register machines—and so we did. The problem was solved."

The power of simplicity.

The Palm Pilot Organizer. This product isn't just a sales success; it's reaching cult status. As *Business Week*[24] reported, at one 1998 meeting of President Clinton's high-tech advisory committee in Santa Clara, CA, 15 of the 22 members whipped out the Palm to schedule future meetings.

What's so stunning is that this product has succeeded where so many have hit the has-been heap—from Sony Corp.'s Magic Link to Apple Computer's Newton. As J. Gerry Purdy, president of market researcher Mobile Insights, observes, "They're a shining star in a grave-yard of miserable failures."

The Palm's formula for success? It was designed for just a few functions so that it's a companion to PCs—not a replacement. That meant giving it the ability to swap new phone numbers or update schedules with a desktop computer at the touch of a button. "Our mantra was simplicity," says Donna Dubinsky, the general manager of 3Com's Palm division. That has earned it a loyal following.

Even all-powerful Microsoft hasn't been able to make up ground. In fact, this is one market where Microsoft may wind up the decided underdog. Despite deep pockets and marketing punch, Windows CE has a handicap: It is so stuffed with features that it takes more steps to handle some key tasks than the 3Com device. That's one reason most experts are betting the Palm will continue to dominate the small-device market for years to come.

The power of simplicity.

Kohl's Department Stores. *Fortune* magazine calls Kohl's "the best retailer you've never heard of." With $3 billion in sales, the company has a rising stock price that is the envy of Sears and Wal-Mart.

As *Fortune* describes Kohl's, "The company is uniquely positioned to please the vast masses who represent Middle America—not too upscale, not too low rent. Like many things about the company, this is simple yet ingenious."[25]

The key to its success is making shopping less of a pain. Sitting on the desk of senior vice president Jim Tinglestad is a sign that reads "No surprises."

That is Kohl's philosophy in a nutshell: no bells, no whistles—just meat and potatoes elevated to high art. "We do 20 simple things that have impact taken together," says COO John Herma. "The key is the consistency of the execution."

The power of simplicity.

The Wine Group. This is another company that you've never heard of. Yet it owns some of the most successful brands in the business. To name a few, *Franzia,* America's best-selling brand; *Corbett Canyon,* America's fastest-growing brand; and *Mogen David,* a very big brand in kosher circles.

When you walk into the very small and very sparse corporate office in San Francisco, you are struck with how simple the Wine Group keeps things.

When you ask Art Ciocca, the CEO, about keeping things simple, he gets very enthusiastic:

"Simplicity is not something organizations tap into automatically. It only works if it's sold from the top down and adopted into the culture of the organization. It helps to have a CEO who likes to keep his own life simple. Personally, I deplore long legal-like documents and rarely read a memo that is more than one page long. Fortunately our business is simple. We still make wine the same way it was made 8,000 years ago.

Yes, we have highly sophisticated computer-driven equipment, but the fundamentals are still the same—making wine better and more efficiently. That is why I seriously question any memo over one page. If an idea can't be expressed on one page, it (or its author) is probably flawed. Although I don't send long memos back anymore, I hope the threat keeps people in our organization thinking smartly and simply.

Today, nearly 25 years later, simplicity is one of the fundamental cornerstones of our company culture and we are one of the largest companies in the wine industry with sales of over 24,000,000 cases. Simplicity played a huge role in getting us here and it works harder for us today than it ever has in the past."

The power of simplicity.

Find/SVP. Andy Garvin found his simple ideas in Paris, working for *Newsweek* magazine. Assigned to write a story on Marcel Bich, founder of the Bic Corporation, Garvin needed a quick briefing. He did what all the magazine's Paris staffers did—he picked up the phone and dialed SVP.

SVP (for s'il vous plait, or "if you please" in French) was a fixture in French business affairs. It was founded on a straightforward premise: When your business has a question, we find the answers.

Andy Garvin was the son and grandson of successful entrepreneurs. The light bulb went on: He could borrow this French concept and adapt it in America. (As we said in Chapter 16, "show me someone else's idea.")

Garvin soaked up details about SVP's operations. He came back to New York with facts, figures, methods, and a licensing deal.

"The concept works because the information that most organizations need already exists," explains Garvin. (How much lamb did New Zealand export last year? Can you explain COBRA in everyday language? Who manufactures digital widgets? That sort of thing.)

"But finding the information is the hassle," says Garvin. "Most people are either in a hurry, or they don't know where to look. We make things simple for them."

The company he founded —Find/SVP—began as a two-person office with six shelf feet of reference material. Today it's a $30 million, publicly traded enterprise with more than 100 consultants.

The power of simplicity.

Charles Industries Ltd. There's no place like home after all. Lots of companies have gone overseas to cut labor and production costs. Charles Industries, a small Midwest company that makes electronics components, was no exception. But as the company grew, it found problems overseas—erratic quality control, higher shipping and inventory costs, erratic customer service.

The simple solution? Move closer to home.

The company closed a plant in the Philippines in favor of expanding one in Marshall, Illinois. It closed another factory in Haiti and moved those operations to Jasonville, Indiana. Then it moved an acquired company's production lines from Nogales, Mexico, to plants in Indiana and Illinois. (In small communities, you can build a factory for about $15 per square foot, compared with $90 in a big metropolitan area.)

Yes, labor costs are higher. But productivity is up and rates of production rejection are way down. Since simplifying things by coming back home, Charles Industries has grown to $100 million in revenues.

The power of simplicity.

Stanislaus Food Products. This is America's "real Italian" tomato company with the Polish name. As we discussed in Chapter 12, the company packs tomatoes and tomato sauce for a large number of those small Italian restaurants all over the United States. It dominates the market. Dino Cortopassi, the CEO, is pretty simpleminded about his approach and his success, "I just want to pack, year in and year out, the best tasting tomato sauce in the business."

If you want lower cost remanufactured sauce (you add water) instead of fresh, he'll lecture you on why what you want makes no sense. If you balk at his higher prices, he'll end the conversation and wish you well. If you call during duck hunting season, you'll have to wait till he comes back.

Dino, by deciding to keep his business simple, does one thing and does it very well. Thus he has simplified his life and made a lot of room for his family and friends and a lot of fun. He does what he wants to do when he wants to do it.

That, ladies and gentlemen, is the power of simplicity.

A SIMPLE SUMMATION

Keep it simple and good things will happen.

Notes

1. Zachary Schiller, "Make It Simple," *Business Week*, September 9, 1996, pp. 96–104.
2. Henry Mintzberg, "Musings on Management," *Harvard Business Review*, July–August 1996, p. 61.
3. Andrew Ferguson, "Now They Want Your Kids," *Time*, September 2, 1997, p. 64.
4. "Jargon Watch," *Fortune*, February 3, 1997, p. 120.
5. Noel Tichy and Ram Charan, "Speed, Simplicity, Self-Confidence: An Interview with Jack Welch," *Harvard Business Review*, September–October 1989, p. 114.
6. Robert Lenzer and Stephens S. Johnson, *Forbes*, "Seeing Thing as They Really Are," March 10, 1997, p. 125.
7. Alan Farnham, "In Search of Suckers," *Fortune*, October 14, 1996, p. 119.
8. John Micklethwait and Adrian Wooldridge, *The Witch Doctors* (New York: Times Books, 1996)..
9. Farnham, "In Search of Suckers."
10. Jeffrey F. Rayport and John J. Sviokla, "Competing in Two Worlds," *McKinsey Quarterly Magazine*.
11. Peter Drucker, *The Effective Executive*, pp. 134–135.
12. Robert J. Dolan and Hermann Simon, *Power Pricing: How Managing Price Transforms the Bottom Line* (New York: Free Press, 1997).
13. Pamela Goett, "Mission Impossible," *Journal of Business Strategy*, January–February 1977, p. 2.
14. Jeffrey Abrahams, *The Mission Statement Book* (Berkeley, Ca: Ten Speed Press, 1995).
15. Jeremy Bullmore, "Was There Life before Mission Statements?" *Marketing Magazine*, July 10, 1997, p. 5.
16. Thomas Petzinger, Jr., "The Frontlines," *The Wall Street Journal*, January 20, 1998, p. B–1.
17. Alex Osborn, *Applied Imagination* (Creative Education Foundation, 1993).
18. March 9, 1998.

19. Jaunary 6, 1998.

20. March 12, 1998.

21. February 23, 1998.

22. Alan Wolfe, "White Magic in America," *The New Republic*, February 23, 1998, pp. 26–34.

23. Ron Zemke, "Embracing the Witch Doctors," *Training Magazine*, July 1997, pp. 41–45.

24. Andy Reinhardt, "Palmy Days for 3Com?" *Business Week*, March 16, 1998, pp. 104–106.

25. Anne Faircloth, "The Best Retailer You've Never Heard Of," *Fortune*, March 16, 1998, pp. 110–112.

Reading List

If you want to learn more about some of the major themes in *The Power of Simplicity*, here's a list of the books that can give you more detail. They are worth reading or at least glancing through.

Adams, Scott. *The Dilbert Principle.* New York: Harper Collins, 1996.

> *Laugh-out-loud funny but dead on when it comes to management fads and other nonsense.*

Drucker, Peter. *The Practice of Management.* New York: Harper & Row, 1954.
———. *The Effective Executive.* New York: Harper Business, 1966.
———. *Managing in a Time of Great Change.* New York: Truman Talley Books, 1995.

> *The fountainhead of common sense and sound advice. Read any one of his dozens of books and you'll be the wiser for it. These are three of our favorites.*

Flesch, Rudolph, *How to Write, Speak and Think More Effectively.* New York: Harper & Row, 1960.

> *The late Dr. Flesch staged a lifelong battle against muddy thinking and murky writing. This is one of his most significant books, packed with examples, exercises, and checklists.*

Micklethwait, John, and Adrian Wooldridge. *The Witch Doctors.* New York: Times Books, 1996.

> *Two staff editors of* The Economist *make sense of the management gurus and debunk a lot of loony thinking. Good sections on the prophets (Peter Drucker), the evangelists (Tom Peters), and the new age preachers (Tony Robbins, Stephen Covey).*

Peppers, Don. *Enterprise One to One*. New York: Doubleday, 1997.

An overly complex but useful look at how to use technology to hang onto your customers.

Ries, Al. *Focus*. New York: HarperCollins, 1996.

Our ex-partner, Al Ries, lays out the case in great detail for doing what a company does best.

Shapiro, Eileen C. *Fad Surfing in the Boardroom*. Reading, Mass.: Addison-Wesley, 1995.

Ms. Shapiro takes deadly aim at the fads that sweep through business like waves in the ocean. Just the "fad dictionary" is worth the price.

Shenk, David. *Data Smog*. New York: HarperCollins, 1997.

We're being smothered by information, and it's dulling our minds. An intelligent look at how to cope with that glut.

Townsend, Robert. *Up the Organization*. New York: Alfred A. Knopf, 1970.

The late Robert Townsend wrote a classic about the foibles of corporations and how to avoid them.

Trout, Jack, and Al Ries. *Marketing Warfare*. New York: McGraw-Hill, 1986.

The bible on how to cope with competition. It will turn you into a killer.

Trout, Jack, and Al Ries. *The 22 Immutable Laws of Marketing*. New York: HarperCollins, 1993.

As we say, violate them at your own risk.

Trout, Jack, and Steve Rivkin. *The New Positioning*. New York: McGraw-Hill, 1995.

Important insights into differentiation and how to build perceptions in the ultimate battleground, the mind of your prospect.

Index

About the Authors

Jack Trout, one of the most famous names in the world of marketing strategy, is president of Trout & Partners. He is a popular speaker and the coauthor of such best-selling business classics as *Positioning*, *The New Positioning*, and *Market Warfare*. Trout's firm consults to such clients as AT&T, IBM, Merck, Southwest Airlines, and Warner-Lambert. He is based in Greenwich, Connecticut.

Steve Rivkin, is coauthor of *The New Positioning* and head of his own communications consulting firm, whose clients include Kraft Foods, Olin Corp., and Horizon Health System. He is based in Glen Rock, New Jersey.